The European Union: A Very Short Introduction

'This up-to-date and accessible guide to the EU, with an authorship team of academic and practitioner experts, will be of benefit to anyone who wants to understand how today's EU works and why it has as many problems as achievements. A very welcome book.'

Alex Warleigh-Lack

'John Pinder writes straightforwardly and beautifully clearly … He has done an extraordinary job of compressing the history, and the book is absolutely up to date.'

Helen Wallace

'John Pinder is in a class of his own. He brings clarity and vision to what is too often complicated and obscure. He causes both friend and foe to wonder what a reformed and strengthened Union could achieve for all Europe and for the wider world.'

Andrew Duff, MEP, Constitutional Affairs Spokesman,
European Liberal Democrats

'… indispensable not only for beginners but for all interested in European issues. Pithy, lucid and accessible it covers recent history, institutions, and policies, as well as future developments.'

Rt. Hon. Giles Radice, MP

'… it not only lives up to but exceeds the promise of its title. This is in fact "The European Union – A Very Short, Useful and Straightforward Guide".'

Independent on Sunday

'invaluable'

William Keegan, Observer

VERY SHORT INTRODUCTIONS are for anyone wanting a stimulating and accessible way in to a new subject. They are written by experts, and have been published in more than 25 languages worldwide.

The series began in 1995, and now represents a wide variety of topics in history, philosophy, religion, science, and the humanities. The VSI library now contains more than 300 volumes—a Very Short Introduction to everything from ancient Egypt and Indian philosophy to conceptual art and cosmology—and will continue to grow in a variety of disciplines.

Very Short Introductions available now:

ADVERTISING Winston Fletcher
AFRICAN HISTORY John Parker and Richard Rathbone
AGNOSTICISM Robin Le Poidevin
AMERICAN IMMIGRATION David A. Gerber
AMERICAN POLITICAL PARTIES AND ELECTIONS L. Sandy Maisel
AMERICAN POLITICS Richard M. Valelly
THE AMERICAN PRESIDENCY Charles O. Jones
ANAESTHESIA Aidan O'Donnell
ANARCHISM Colin Ward
ANCIENT EGYPT Ian Shaw
ANCIENT GREECE Paul Cartledge
ANCIENT PHILOSOPHY Julia Annas
ANCIENT WARFARE Harry Sidebottom
ANGELS David Albert Jones
ANGLICANISM Mark Chapman
THE ANGLO-SAXON AGE John Blair
THE ANIMAL KINGDOM Peter Holland
ANIMAL RIGHTS David DeGrazia
THE ANTARCTIC Klaus Dodds
ANTISEMITISM Steven Beller
ANXIETY Daniel Freeman and Jason Freeman
THE APOCRYPHAL GOSPELS Paul Foster
ARCHAEOLOGY Paul Bahn
ARCHITECTURE Andrew Ballantyne
ARISTOCRACY William Doyle
ARISTOTLE Jonathan Barnes

ART HISTORY Dana Arnold
ART THEORY Cynthia Freeland
ATHEISM Julian Baggini
AUGUSTINE Henry Chadwick
AUSTRALIA Kenneth Morgan
AUTISM Uta Frith
THE AVANT GARDE David Cottington
THE AZTECS David Carrasco
BACTERIA Sebastian G.B. Amyes
BARTHES Jonathan Culler
BEAUTY Roger Scruton
BESTSELLERS John Sutherland
THE BIBLE John Riches
BIBLICAL ARCHAEOLOGY Eric H. Cline
BIOGRAPHY Hermione Lee
THE BLUES Elijah Wald
THE BOOK OF MORMON Terryl Givens
BORDERS Alexander C. Diener and Joshua Hagen
THE BRAIN Michael O'Shea
THE BRITISH CONSTITUTION Martin Loughlin
THE BRITISH EMPIRE Ashley Jackson
BRITISH POLITICS Anthony Wright
BUDDHA Michael Carrithers
BUDDHISM Damien Keown
THE BRITISH EMPIRE Ashly Jackson
BUDDHIST ETHICS Damien Keown
CANCER Nicholas James
CAPITALISM James Fulcher
CATHOLICISM Gerald O'Collins

For more information visit our website
www.oup.com/vsi/

John Pinder and Simon Usherwood

THE EUROPEAN
UNION

A Very Short Introduction

OXFORD
UNIVERSITY PRESS

OXFORD
UNIVERSITY PRESS

Great Clarendon Street, Oxford, OX2 6DP,
United Kingdom

Oxford University Press is a department of the University of Oxford.
It furthers the University's objective of excellence in research, scholarship,
and education by publishing worldwide. Oxford is a registered trade mark of
Oxford University Press in the UK and in certain other countries

© John Pinder and Simon Usherwood 2013

The moral rights of the authors have been asserted

First Edition published in 2001
Second Edition published in 2007
This Edition published 2013

Impression: 1

Published in the United States of America by Oxford University Press
198 Madison Avenue, New York, NY 10016, United States of America

British Library Cataloguing in Publication Data

Data available

ISBN 978-0-19-968169-3

Printed in Great Britain by
Ashford Colour Press Ltd, Gosport, Hampshire

Contents

The European Union

Preface

To encapsulate an entity such as the European Union within such a brief book continues to be a real challenge as we enter our third edition. In part, this reflects our desire not only to set out the fundamentals of the European integration process, but also to make an argument about the need for that integration. In part, it is the result of the nature of Union itself, which has come to play such a vital role in contemporary European governance.

Whatever the reason, we have sought to build on our (very different) experiences and understandings. John, who was the sole author of the first edition, has been following developments for well over half a century. He formed the view very early on that it would be best to move by steps and stages in a federal direction and has seen no reason to change it. This does not mean pulling up the old nations of Europe by the roots and trying to plant them in virgin soil, but developing a framework in which they can deal with their common problems in an effective and democratic way. His choice of ideas is inevitably coloured by this view. Simon's experience has drawn on the post-Maastricht era, with all the difficulties of building constitutional frameworks and involving citizens that this has brought. He, too, recognizes the value of federalism as a guiding principle for integration, albeit in a system where states are likely to remain central actors for the foreseeable future.

The concern of both of us has been to present the ideas in a way that will help to provide a context for reasonable people, whether they lean towards a federal or an intergovernmental approach, to evaluate the performance of the Union and judge in which direction it should go. And we have endeavoured to be scrupulous about the facts.

It would be an understatement to say that the Union has seen much happen in the five years since the second edition, and we have endeavoured to reflect those changes and challenges throughout the text. As before, we owe thanks to many people, including Iain Begg, Laura Chappell, Brendan Connelly, Andrew Duff, Roberta Guerrina, Nigel Haigh, Christopher Johnson, Jörg Monar, and Simon Nuttall; while those responsible at OUP combined efficiency with understanding of authors' needs. If what follows does not please the reader, it is no fault of theirs.

January 2013

John Pinder
Simon Usherwood

Abbreviations

ACP	African, Caribbean, Pacific countries
AFSJ	area of freedom, security, and justice
ALDE	Alliance of Liberals and Democrats for Europe
Benelux	Belgium, Netherlands, and Luxembourg
BRIC	Brazil, Russia, India, and China
CAP	common agricultural policy
CFCs	chlorofluorocarbons
CFSP	Common Foreign and Security Policy
CIS	Commonwealth of Independent States
CJHA	Cooperation in Justice and Home Affairs
Comecon	Council for Mutual Economic Assistance
Coreper	Committee of Permanent Representatives
CSDP	Common Security and Defence Policy
EAGGF	European Agricultural Guidance and Guarantee Fund
EC	European Community
ECB	European Central Bank
ECJ	European Court of Justice (formal title, Court of Justice)
Ecofin	Council of Economic and Finance Ministers
Ecosoc	Economic and Social Committee
ECR	European Conservatives and Reformists
ECSC	European Coal and Steel Community
ecu	European Currency Unit (forerunner of euro)
EDC	European Defence Community
EDF	European Development Fund

EEA	European Economic Area
EEC	European Economic Community
EFA	European Free Alliance
EFD	Europe of Freedom and Democracy
EFSF	European Financial Stability Fund
Efta	European Free Trade Association
ELDR	European Liberals, Democrats, and Reformists
EMS	European Monetary System
Emu	Economic and Monetary Union
ENP	European Neighbourhood Policy
EPC	European Political Cooperation
EPP–ED	European People's Party and European Democrats
ERDF	European Regional Development Fund
ERM	Exchange Rate Mechanism
ESCB	European System of Central Banks
ESDP	European Security and Defence Policy
ESF	European Social Fund
ESM	European Stability Mechanism
ETS	Emissions Trading Scheme
EU	European Union
Euratom	European Atomic Energy Community
Gatt	General Agreement on Tariffs and Trade (forerunner of WTO)
GDP	Gross Domestic Product
GNI	Gross National Income
GNP	Gross National Product
GSP	Generalized System of Preferences
GUE/NGL	European United Left/Nordic Green Left
IGC	Intergovernmental Conference
Ind	Independent
MEP	Member of the European Parliament
Nato	North Atlantic Treaty Organization
NTBs	non-tariff barriers
OECD	Organization for Economic Cooperation and Development
OLP	Ordinary Legislative Procedure
OMC	Open method of coordination
OSCE	Organization for Security and Cooperation in Europe

PES	Party of European Socialists
PHARE	Poland and Hungary: aid for economic reconstruction (extended to other Central and East European countries)
QMV	qualified majority voting (in the Council)
SEA	Single European Act
SGP	Stability and Growth Pact
TACIS	Technical Assistance to the CIS
TEC	Treaty establishing the European Community
TEU	Treaty on European Union
TFEU	Treaty on the Functioning of the European Union
TSCG	Treaty on Stability, Coordination, and Governance in the Economic and Monetary Union
UN	United Nations
UNFCCC	UN Framework Convention on Climate Change
VAT	value-added tax
WEU	Western European Union
WTO	World Trade Organization

List of boxes

List of Boxes

List of charts

List of illustrations

The publisher and the authors apologize for any errors or omissions in the above list. If contacted they will be pleased to rectify these at the earliest opportunity.

List of maps

Chapter 1
What the EU is for

The European Union of today is the result of a process that began over half a century ago with the creation of the European Coal and Steel Community. Those two industries then still provided the industrial muscle for military power; and Robert Schuman, the French Foreign Minister, affirmed on 9 May 1950 in his declaration which launched the project that 'any war between France and Germany' would become 'not merely unthinkable, but materially impossible'. The award of the 2012 Nobel Prize for Peace to the European Union represents the importance of that very process.

A durable peace

It may not be easy, at today's distance, to appreciate how much this meant, only five years after the end of the war of 1939–45 that had brought such terrible suffering to almost all European countries. For France and Germany, which had been at war with each other three times in the preceding eight decades, finding a way to live together in a durable peace was a fundamental political priority that the new Community was designed to serve.

For France the prospect of a completely independent Germany, with its formidable industrial potential, was alarming. The attempt to keep Germany down, as the French had tried to do after the 1914–18 war, had failed disastrously. The idea of binding Germany within strong institutions, which would equally bind France and other European countries and thus be acceptable to Germans over the longer term, seemed more promising. That promise has been amply fulfilled. The French could regard the European Union (EU) as the outcome of their original initiative, and they sought, with considerable success, to play the part of a leader among European nations, though since the accession of 12 new member states in 2005 and 2007, they have become less confident of their leadership role.

But participation in these European institutions on an equal basis has also given Germany a framework within which to develop peaceful and constructive relations with the growing number of other member states, as well as to complete their unification smoothly in 1990. Following the 12 years of Nazi rule that ended with devastation in 1945, the Community offered Germans a way to become a respected people again. The idea of a Community of equals with strong institutions was attractive. Schuman had also declared that the new Community would be 'the first concrete foundation of a European federation which is indispensable to the preservation of peace'. But whereas French commitment to developing the Community in a federal direction has been variable, the German political class, having thoroughly absorbed the concept of federal democracy, has quite consistently supported such development. In 1992, indeed, an amendment to the Basic Law of the reunited Germany provided for its participation in the European Union committed to federal principles.

The other four founder states, Belgium, Italy, Luxembourg, and the Netherlands, also saw the new Community as a means to ensure peace by binding Germany within strong European institutions. For the most part they too, like the Germans, saw the Community as a stage in the development of a federal polity and have largely continued to do so.

Although World War Two is receding into a more distant past, the motive of peace and security within a democratic polity that was fundamental to the foundation of the Community remains a powerful influence on governments and politicians in many of the member states. The system that has provided a framework for over half a century of peace is regarded as a guarantee of future stability. One example was the decision to consolidate it by introducing the single currency, seen as a way to reinforce the safe anchorage of the potentially more powerful Germany after its unification; the accession of ten Central and East European states, seeking a safe haven after World War Two followed by half a century of Soviet domination, was another; and there has been continuing pressure to strengthen the Union's institutions in order to maintain stability as eastern enlargement increases the number of member states towards 30 or more, including several new democracies.

The British, having avoided the experience of defeat and occupation, did not share that fundamental motive for the sharing of sovereignty with other European peoples and felt reliance on the US and Nato to be sufficient. Hence the focus on the economic aspects of integration that has been common among British politicians and has restricted their ability to play an influential and constructive part in some of the most significant developments. The EU's potential contribution to making the world a safer place in fields such as climate change and peacekeeping, as well as with its external economic and aid policies more generally, could, however, as suggested later in this book, provide grounds for a change in this fundamental British attitude.

Economic strength and prosperity

While a durable peace was a profound political motive for establishing the new Community, it would not have succeeded without adequate performance in the economic field in which it was given its powers; and the Community did in fact serve economic as well as political logic. The frontiers between France, Germany, Belgium, and Luxembourg, standing between steel plants and the mines whose coal they required, impeded rational production; and the removal of those barriers, accompanied by common governance of the resulting common market, was successful in economic terms. This, together with the evidence that peaceful reconciliation among the member states was being achieved, encouraged them to see the European Coal and Steel Community as a first step, as Schuman had indicated, in a process of political as well as economic unification. After an unsuccessful attempt at a second step, when the French National Assembly failed to ratify a treaty for a European Defence Community in 1954, the six founder states proceeded again on the path of economic integration. The concept of the common market was extended to the whole of their mutual trade in goods when the European Economic Community (EEC) was founded in 1958, opening up the way to an integrated economy that responded to the logic of economic interdependence among the member states.

The EEC was also, thanks to French insistence on surrounding the common market with a common external tariff, able to enter trade negotiations on level terms with the United States; and this demonstrated the potential of the Community to become a major actor in the international system when it has a common instrument with which to conduct an external policy. It was a first step towards satisfying another motive for creating the Community: to restore European influence in the wider world, which had been dissipated by the two great fratricidal wars, and which can now be reinforced by the Union's potential for contributing to much-needed global safety and prosperity.

One exception to the British failure to understand the strength of the case for such radical reform was Winston Churchill who, less than a year and a half after the end of the war, said in a speech in Zurich: 'We must now build a kind of United States of Europe...the first step must be a partnership between France and Germany...France and Germany must take the lead together.' But few among the British understood so well the case for a new Community, and Churchill himself did not feel that Britain, then at the head of its Empire and with a recently forged special relationship with the United States, should be a member. Many were, however, reluctant to be disadvantaged in Continental markets and excluded from the taking of important policy decisions. So after failing to secure a free trade area that would incorporate the EEC as well as other West European countries, successive British governments sought entry into the Community, finally succeeding in 1973. But while the British played a leading part in developing the common market into a more complete single market, they continued to lack the political motives that

1. Churchill at The Hague: founds the European Movement, following his call for 'a kind of United States of Europe'

have driven the founder states, as well as some others, to press towards other forms of deeper integration.

It is important to understand the motives of the founders and of the British which, while they continue to evolve, still influence attitudes towards the European Union. Such motives are shared, in various proportions, by other states which have acceded over the years; and they underlie much of the drama that has unfolded since 1950 to produce the Union which is the subject of this book.

Theories and explanations

There are two main ways of explaining the phenomenon of the Community and the Union. Adherents to one emphasize the role of the member states and their intergovernmental dealings; adherents to the other give greater weight to the European institutions.

Most of the former, belonging to the 'realist' or 'neo-realist' schools of thought, hold that the Community and the Union have not wrought any fundamental change in the relationships among the member states, whose governments continue to pursue their national interests and seek to maximize their power within the EU as elsewhere. A more recent variant, called liberal intergovernmentalism, looks to the play of forces in their domestic politics to explain the governments' behaviour in the Union. For want of a better word, 'intergovernmentalist' is used below for this family of explanations as to how the Community and Union work.

One should not underestimate the role that the governments retain in the Union's affairs, with their status as the signatories of the Union's treaties, their power of decision in the Council that represents the member states, and their monopoly of the *ultima ratio* of armed force. But other approaches, including those known as neo-functionalism and federalism, give more weight than the intergovernmentalists to the European institutions.

Neo-functionalists saw the Community developing by a process of 'spillover' from the original ECSC, with its scope confined to only two industrial sectors. Interest groups and political parties, attracted by the success of the Community in dealing with the problems of these two sectors, would become frustrated by its inability to deal with related problems in other fields and would, with leadership from the European Commission, press successfully for the Community's competence to be extended, until it would eventually provide a form of European governance for a wide range of the affairs of the member states. This offers at least a partial explanation of some steps in the Community's development, including the move from the single market to the single currency.

A federalist perspective, while also stressing the importance of the common institutions, goes beyond neo-functionalism in two main ways. First, it relates the transfer of powers to the Union less to a spillover from existing powers to new ones than to the growing inability of governments to deal effectively with problems that have become transnational and so escape the reach of existing states. Most of these problems concern the economy, the environment, and security; and the states should retain control over matters with which they can still cope adequately. Second, whereas neo-functionalists have not been clear about the principles that would shape the European institutions, a federalist perspective is based on principles of liberal democracy: in particular, the rule of law based on fundamental rights, and representative government with the laws enacted and the executive controlled by elected representatives of the citizens. In this view, the powers exercised jointly need to be dealt with by institutions of government, because the intergovernmental method is neither effective nor democratic enough to satisfy the needs of citizens of democratic states. So either the federal elements in the institutions will be strengthened until the Union becomes an effective democratic polity, based on the principles of rule of law and representative government; or it will fail to attract enough support from the citizens to enable it to flourish, and perhaps even to survive. The Union is not designed to replace member states, but rather to transform them into integral parts of a cooperative venture: citizens' identities gain a new layer that interacts with their existing ones.

Subsequent chapters will try to show how far the development of the Community and the Union has reflected these different views. Meanwhile the reader should be warned: the authors consider that the need for effective and democratic government has moved the EC and the EU by steps and stages quite far in a federal direction and should, but by no means certainly will, continue to do so.

Chapter 2
How the EU was made

'Europe will not be made all at once, or according to a single, general plan. It will be built through concrete achievements, which first create a de facto solidarity.' With these words, the Schuman declaration accurately predicted the way in which the Community has become the Union of today. The institutions and powers have been developed step by step, following the confidence gained through the success of preceding steps, to deal with matters that appeared to be best handled by common action.

Subsequent chapters consider particular institutions and fields of competence in more detail. Here we see how interests and events combined to bring about the development as a whole. Some primary interests and motives were considered in the previous chapter: security, not just through military means but by establishing economic and political relationships; prosperity, with business and trade unions particularly interested; protection of the environment, with pressure from green parties and voluntary organizations, and with climate change a matter of increasingly general concern; and influence in external relations, to promote common interests in the wider world.

With the creation of the Community to serve such purposes, other interests came into play. Those who feared damage from certain aspects sought compensation through redistributive measures: for France, the common agricultural policy to counterbalance German industrial advantage; the structural funds for countries with weaker economies, which feared they would lose from the single market; budgetary adjustments for the British and others with high net contributions. Some governments, parliaments, parties, and voluntary organizations have pressed for reforms aiming to make the institutions more effective and democratic. Against them have stood those who resist moves beyond intergovernmental decision-making, acting from a variety of motives: ideological commitment to the nation-state; a belief that democracy is feasible only within and not beyond it; mistrust of foreigners; and simple attachment to the status quo. Among them have been such historic figures as President de Gaulle and Prime Minister Thatcher, as well as a wide range of institutions and individuals, most prevalent among the British, Danes, Czechs, and Poles. Among the European institutions, it is the Council of Ministers that has come closest to this view.

Two of the most influential federalists, committed to the development of a European polity that would deal effectively with the common interests of the member states and their citizens, have been Jean Monnet and Jacques Delors. Both initiated major steps towards a federal aim. Altiero Spinelli represented a different kind of federalism, envisaging more radical moves towards a European constitution. The German, Italian, Belgian, and Dutch parliaments and governments have in varying degrees been institutionally federalist, as have the European Commission and Parliament, and, in so far as the treaties could be interpreted in that way, the Court of Justice. They have generally preferred Monnet's stepwise approach, although the Belgians, Italians, and European Parliament have espoused constitutional federalism.

1950s: the founding treaties

Monnet was responsible for drafting the Schuman declaration, chaired the negotiations for the ECSC Treaty, and was the first President of its High Authority. These two words reflected his insistence on a strong executive at the centre of the Community, stemming originally from his experience as Deputy Secretary General of the interwar League of Nations which convinced him of the weakness of an intergovernmental system. He was, however, persuaded that, for democratic member states, such a Community should be provided with a parliamentary assembly and a court— embryonic elements of a federal legislature and judiciary—and that there should be a council of ministers of the member states.

This structure has remained remarkably stable to this day, though the relationship between the institutions has changed: the Council, and in particular, since 1974, the European Council of government heads, has become the most powerful; the European Commission, while still very important, has lost ground to it; the European Parliament has gained in power; and the Court of Justice has established itself as the supreme judicial authority in matters of Community competence. Although they were later to accept these institutions, British governments of the 1950s felt them to be too federal for British participation.

2. Monnet (left) and Schuman (right)

Le 6 Mai 1950

La paix mondiale ne saurait être sauvegardée sans des efforts créateurs à la mesure des dangers qui la menacent.

La contribution qu'une Europe organisée et vivante peut apporter à la civilisation est indispensable au maintien des relations pacifiques. En se faisant depuis plus de 20 ans le champion d'une Europe unie, la France a toujours eu pour objet essentiel de servir la paix. L'Europe n'a pas été faite, nous avons eu la guerre.

L'Europe ne se fera pas d'un coup, ni dans une construction d'ensemble : elle se fera par des réalisations concrètes créant d'abord une solidarité de fait. Le rassemblement des nations européennes exige que l'opposition séculaire de la France et de l'Allemagne soit éliminée : l'action entreprise doit toucher au premier chef la France et l'Allemagne.

Dans ce but, le Gouvernement Français propose de porter immédiatement l'action sur un point limité mais décisif :

Le Gouvernement Français propose de placer l'ensemble de la production franco-allemande de charbon et d'acier, sous une Haute Autorité commune, dans une organisation ouverte à la participation des autres pays d'Europe.

La mise en commun des productions de charbon et d'acier assurera immédiatement l'établissement de bases communes de développement économique, première étape de la Fédération européenne, et changera le destin de ces régions longtemps vouées à la fabrication des armes de guerre dont elles ont été les plus constantes victimes.

3. Page one of the text Monnet sent to Schuman for his Declaration of 9 May 1950

The six member states, however, were minded to proceed further in that direction. The French government reacted to American insistence on German rearmament, following the impact of communist expansionism in both Europe and Korea, by proposing a European Defence Community with a European army. An EDC Treaty was signed by the six governments and ratified by four; but opposition grew in France and the Assemblée Nationale voted in 1954 to shelve it. The result was that the idea of a competence in the field of defence remained a no-go area until the 1990s.

While the collapse of the EDC was a severe setback, confidence in the Community as a framework for peaceful relations among the member states had grown; and there was a powerful political impulse to 'relaunch' its development. The Dutch were ready with a proposal for a general common market, for which the support of Belgium and Germany was soon forthcoming. The French, still markedly protectionist, were doubtful. But they held to the project of European unification built around Franco-German partnership and so accepted the common market which the Germans wanted, on condition that other French interests were satisfied: an atomic energy community in which France was equipped to play the leading part; the common agricultural policy; the association of colonial territories on favourable terms; and equal pay for women throughout the Community, without which French industry, already required by French law to pay it, would in some sectors have been at a competitive disadvantage. The Italians for their part, who had the weakest economy among the six, secured the European Investment Bank, the Social Fund, and free movement of labour. So all these elements were included in the two Rome Treaties, which established the European Economic Community (EEC) and European Atomic Energy Community (Euratom): an early example of a package deal, incorporating advantages for each member state, which has characterized many of the steps taken since then.

The two new treaties entered into force on 1 January 1958. While Euratom was sidelined, the EEC became the basis for the future development of the Community. Its institutions were similar to those of the ECSC, though with a somewhat less powerful executive, called Commission instead of High Authority; and the EEC was given a wide range of economic competences, including the power to establish a customs union with internal free trade

Box 1 The Treaties

Rome wasn't built in a day; and the Treaties of Rome (in force in 1958) were a big building block in a long and complicated process that has constructed the present European Union. Other major treaties included the ECSC Treaty (in force 1952), Single European Act (1987), Maastricht Treaty (1993), Amsterdam Treaty (1999), Nice Treaty (2002), and Lisbon Treaty (2009).

A minor complication is that there were two Treaties of Rome (see below), but the EEC Treaty was so much more important than the Euratom Treaty that it is generally known as *the* Treaty of Rome.

A major complication is that the European Union was set up by the Maastricht Treaty, with two new 'pillars' for foreign policy and internal security alongside the European Community, which already had its own treaties. These were organized alongside the EC Treaty (TEC), within the EU Treaty (TEU). The Lisbon Treaty finally produced some simplification of this, by collapsing all the pillars into one: the EU now operates on the basis of the TEU and the Treaty on the Functioning of the European Union (TFEU).

N.B. to avoid undue complexity, this book follows two principles in referring to the EC and EU:

- European Community, Community, or EC is used regarding matters relating entirely to the time before the EU was established, or in the period between Maastricht and Lisbon when the EC's separate characteristics are relevant;

- European, Union, or EU in all other cases.

and a common external tariff; policies for particular sectors, notably agriculture; and more general cooperation.

The first President of the Commission, Walter Hallstein, led the Commission into a flying start, with acceleration of the timetable for establishing the customs union; and within this framework the Community enjoyed notable economic success in the 1960s, with growth averaging some 5 per cent a year, twice as fast as in Britain and the United States. But conflict between the emergent federal Community, as conceived by Monnet or Hallstein, and de Gaulle's fundamentalist commitment to the nation-state made that decade politically hazardous for the Community.

The 1960s: de Gaulle against the federalists

In June 1958, less than six months after the Rome Treaties came into force, de Gaulle became French President. He did not like the federal elements and aspirations of the Community. But nor was he prepared to challenge directly treaties recently ratified by France. He sought, rather, to use the Community as a means to advance French power and leadership. One example was his sidelining of Euratom in order to keep the French atomic sector national. Another was his veto which terminated in 1963 the first negotiations to enlarge the Community to include Britain, Denmark, Ireland, and Norway. Although the British government's conception of the Community was closer to that of de Gaulle than of the other, more federalist-minded member states' governments, and Britain's defence of its agricultural and Commonwealth interests had irked them by making the negotiations hard and long, they resented the unilateral and nationalist manner of the veto so deeply that it provoked the first political crisis within the Community. This was followed, in 1965, by a greater crisis over the arrangements for the common agricultural policy (CAP).

The CAP had from the outset been a key French interest and de Gaulle was determined to have it established without undue delay. It was to be based on price supports requiring substantial public expenditure. Both France and the Commission agreed that this should come from the budget of the Community, not the member states. But the Commission, with its federalist orientation, and the

Dutch parliament, with its deep commitment to democratic principles, insisted that the budget spending must be subject to parliamentary control; and since a European budget could not be controlled by six separate parliaments, it would have to be done by the European Parliament. This suited the other governments well enough, but was anathema to de Gaulle. He precipitated the crisis of 'the empty chair', forbidding his ministers to attend meetings of the Council throughout the second half of 1965 and evoking fears among the other states that he might be preparing to destroy the Community.

Neither side was willing to give way and the episode concluded in January 1966 with the so-called 'Luxembourg compromise'. The French government asserted a right of veto when interests 'very important to one or more member states' are at stake; and the other five affirmed their commitment to the treaty provision for qualified majority voting on certain questions, which was that very month due to come into effect for votes on a wide range of subjects. In practice de Gaulle's view prevailed for the next two decades, so that Luxembourg 'veto' seems a more accurate description than 'compromise'. In the mid-1980s, however, majority voting began to be practised in the context of the single market programme, and has now become the standard procedure applicable to most legislative decisions.

Despite these conflicts between the intergovernmental and the federal conceptions, the customs union was completed by July 1968, earlier than the treaty required. Its impact had already been felt not only internally but also in the Community's external relations. Wielding the common instrument of the external tariff, the Community was becoming, in the field of trade, a power comparable to the United States. President Kennedy had reacted by proposing multilateral negotiations for major tariff cuts. Skilfully led by the Commission, the Community responded positively; and the outcome was cuts averaging one-third, initiating an era in which it was to become the major force for international trade liberalization.

Alongside the ups and downs of Community politics, the Court of Justice made steady progress in establishing the rule of law. Based on its treaty obligation to ensure that 'the law is observed', in judgments in 1963 and 1964 the Court established the principles of the primacy and the direct effect of Community law, so that it would be consistently applied in all the member states. Though without the means of enforcement proper to a state, respect for the law, based on the treaties and on legislation enacted by its institutions, provided cement that has bound the Community together.

Widening and some deepening: Britain, Denmark, Ireland join

With de Gaulle's resignation in 1969, French policy became more pragmatic. Britain, Denmark, Ireland, and Norway still sought entry; and the new President, Georges Pompidou, consented, on condition of agreeing CAP financing, as well as elements of 'deepening' such as monetary union and coordination of foreign policy. In addition to serving the French agricultural interest, these were intended to integrate Germany yet more firmly into the Community, as well as guard against the danger that widening the Community would weaken it. This fitted well with the strategic outlook of the German Chancellor, Willy Brandt, who was simultaneously opening to the Soviet bloc with Ostpolitik and binding Germany into the West with his plans for enlargement and monetary union.

However, economic and monetary union would have to wait, as German desires for strong coordination of economic policy were a step too far for the French. The result was a system for cooperation on exchange rates that was too weak to survive the international currency turbulence of that period. Similarly, the system devised for foreign policy cooperation was strictly intergovernmental: this limited its impact. While France was able to secure a very favourable financial regulation for CAP, this was balanced by giving the European Parliament the power to share control of the budget with the Council, a decision consolidated in treaties in 1970 and 1975. While this was just a foot in the door to budgetary powers for the Parliament, it was to grow into a major element in the Union's institutional structure.

Britain, together with Denmark and Ireland, joined the Community in January 1973, though the Norwegians rejected accession in a referendum. The British too were to vote in a referendum in 1975. Harold Wilson had replaced Edward Heath as Prime Minister in 1974 following an election victory by the Labour Party, which was turning more and more against the Community (a position that lasted into the 1980s). After a somewhat cosmetic 'renegotiation', the Wilson government did recommend continued membership; and in 1975 the voters approved it by a two-to-one majority. With Margaret Thatcher's Conservatives coming to power in 1979, a new line of tension was opened, as she fought to 'get our money back', as she put it, by blocking much Community business until she secured agreement in 1984 to reduce Britain's high net contribution to the Community's budget.

As so often in the EU's history, the 1970s saw the simultaneous development of both intergovernmental and supranational activities. French President Valéry Giscard d'Estaing, a Gaullist by tradition, launched both regular meetings of the European Council between national leaders, as well as direct elections to the European Parliament. The European Council was soon to play a central part in taking Community decisions, settling conflicts that ministers in the Council were unable to resolve, and agreeing on major package deals. Provision had already been made for direct elections in the treaties of the 1950s, but it was only now that governments agreed and the first elections were held in June 1979. This step towards representative democracy was to have a big impact on the Community's future development. Of similar importance, 1979 also saw the creation of a system of

4. British entry: Heath signs the Treaty of Accession

exchange-rate stabilization—the European Monetary System (EMS)—which was to shape later discussions on monetary union.

Single market, Draft Treaty on European Union, southern enlargement

Jacques Delors became President of the Commission in January 1985. He had visited each member state to find out what major project was likely to be accepted by all of them. As a federalist in Monnet's tradition, his short-list contained projects—single market, single currency, common defence policy, institutional reform—that could be seen as steps in a federal direction. But Thatcher, whose view of federalism was akin to de Gaulle's, and so was hostile to the currency, defence, and institutional projects, was at the same time a militant economic liberal who saw the single market as an important measure of trade liberalization. European economies had lost momentum during the hard times of the 1970s and all the governments accepted the single market project as a way to break out of what was then called eurosclerosis. The project was strongly backed by the more dynamic firms and the main business associations, especially since the Luxembourg 'compromise' had served to let non-tariff barriers to trade build up during the period.

The successful abolition of tariffs on internal trade had demonstrated the value of a programme with a timetable. So the Commission produced a list of some 300 measures to be enacted by the end of 1992 in order to complete the single market by removing the non-tariff barriers. The Commissioner in charge of the project was Lord Cockfield, a former minister in the Thatcher

5. Delors: single market, single currency, single-minded European

government; and the programme was rapidly drafted in time to be presented to the European Council in Milan in June 1985.

Meanwhile the European Parliament had prepared a political project: a Draft Treaty on European Union, inspired by Altiero Spinelli, the leading figure since the 1950s among those federalists who saw the drafting of a constitution as the royal road to federation. The Draft Treaty was designed to reform the Community's institutions so as to give them a federal character; to extend its powers to include most of those that would be normal in a federation, with the key exception of defence; and to come into effect when ratified by a majority of the member states, with suitable arrangements to be negotiated with any states that did not ratify. While there was widespread support for the draft in most of the founder states, the German government was among those that were not prepared to countenance the probable exclusion of Britain. President Mitterrand did, however, express support for the draft, albeit in somewhat equivocal terms; and its main proposals were presented to the European Council in Milan along with the Commission's single market project.

The European Council decided to convene an Intergovernmental Conference (IGC) on treaty amendment, overriding British, Danish, and Greek opposition with its first-ever use of a majority vote. The IGC considered amendments relating not only to the single market programme but also to a number of the proposals in the Parliament's Draft Treaty. The outcome was the Single European Act, which provided for completion of the single market by 1992; gave the Community competences in the fields of the environment, technological research and development, social policies relating to employment, and 'cohesion'; and brought foreign policy cooperation into the Treaty's architecture (albeit with the retention of distinct intergovernmental procedures)—hence the title Single European Act, to distinguish it from a proposal to keep foreign policy separate. The Single Act also provided for qualified majority voting in a number of areas of

6. Spinelli voting for his Draft Treaty on European Union

single market legislation, and strengthened the European
Parliament through a 'cooperation procedure' which gave it
influence over such legislation, together with a procedure
requiring its assent to treaties of association and accession.

The Community was enlarged in 1981 to include Greece and, in
1986, Portugal and Spain. All three had been ruled by
authoritarian regimes and saw the Community as a support for
their democracies as well as for economic modernization. The
Community for its part wanted them to be viable member states
and to be supportive of its projects, such as the single market. It
was to this end that the cohesion policy, based on a doubling of
the structural funds for assisting the development of economically
weaker regions, was included in the Single Act.

Thus the Single Act strengthened both the Community's powers and its institutions, with influence from a combination of governments, economic interests, social concerns, the Commission, the Parliament, and a variety of federalist forces. It was succeeded by the Maastricht, Amsterdam, Nice, and Lisbon Treaties, likewise strengthening both powers and institutions, and responding to similar combinations of pressures. This would not have happened had the Single Act not been successful. But the prospect of the single market helped to revive the economy, and the Community institutions gained in strength as they dealt with the vast programme of legislation.

Spinelli died a few weeks after the signing of the Single Act under the impression that it was a failure: 'a dead mouse', as he put it. In fact it initiated a relaunching of the Community which may have been as far-reaching in its effects as that which led to the Treaties of Rome.

Maastricht and Amsterdam Treaties, enlargement from 12 to 15

Following his success with the single market, Delors was determined to pursue the project of the single currency. Thatcher had not been alone in opposing it. Most Germans, proud of the Deutschmark as the Community's strongest currency, were decidedly unenthusiastic. But it remained a major French objective, for economic as well as political reasons; and Helmut Kohl, a long-standing federalist, held that it would be a crucial step towards a federal Europe. While he facilitated the preparation of plans for the single currency, however, he faced difficulty in securing the necessary support in Germany.

The events of 1989 were a seismic upheaval. With the disintegration of the Soviet bloc, which opened up the prospect of enlarging the Community to the East, German unification also became possible. But Kohl needed Mitterrand's support: both for

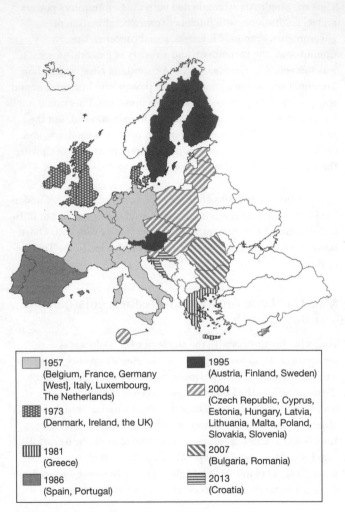

▨ 1957 (Belgium, France, Germany [West], Italy, Luxembourg, The Netherlands)	■ 1995 (Austria, Finland, Sweden)
▦ 1973 (Denmark, Ireland, the UK)	▨ 2004 (Czech Republic, Cyprus, Estonia, Hungary, Latvia, Lithuania, Malta, Poland, Slovakia, Slovenia)
▥ 1981 (Greece)	▨ 2007 (Bulgaria, Romania)
▦ 1986 (Spain, Portugal)	▤ 2013 (Croatia)

Map 1. Growth of the EU, 1957–2013

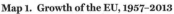

formal reasons because France, as an occupying power, had the right to veto German unification; and, pursuing the policy initiated by Brandt, to ensure that new eastern relationships did not undermine the European Community and the Franco-German partnership. Mitterrand saw the single currency as the way to anchor Germany irrevocably in the Community system, and hence as a condition for German unification; and this ensured for Kohl the necessary support in Germany to proceed with the project.

The result was the Maastricht Treaty, which provided not only for the euro and the European Central Bank but also for other competences and institutional reforms. The Community was given some powers in the fields of education, youth, culture, and public health. Its institutions were strengthened in a number of ways, including more scope for qualified majority voting in the Council. The role of the European Parliament was enhanced through a 'co-decision' procedure that required its approval as well as that of the Council for laws in a number of fields; and it secured the right to approve—or not—the appointment of each new Commission. Two new 'pillars' were set up alongside the Community: one for a 'common foreign and security policy'; the other, relating to freedom of movement and internal security, for what was called 'cooperation in justice and home affairs'—renamed in the Amsterdam Treaty as 'police and judicial cooperation in criminal matters'. The basis for both was intergovernmental, though they were related to the Community institutions. The whole unwieldy structure was named the European Union, with the first, central, Community pillar as well as the other two.

Although John Major had succeeded Mrs Thatcher as Prime Minister with the avowed intention of moving to 'the heart of Europe', he insisted that Britain would participate neither in the single currency nor in a 'social chapter' on matters relating to employment. In order to secure agreement on the treaty as a whole, it was accepted that Britain could opt out of both, together with Denmark as far as the single currency was concerned.

The Maastricht Treaty was signed in February 1992 and entered into force in November 1993 after a number of vicissitudes: two Danish referendums, in the first of which it was rejected and in the second approved after some small adjustments had been made; a French referendum in which the voters accepted it by a tiny majority; in London, a fraught ratification process in the House of Commons; and in Germany, a lengthy deliberation by the Constitutional Court before it rejected a claim that the treaty was unconstitutional. These episodes, together with evidence that citizens' approval of the Union was declining in most member states, seemed alarming, particularly to people of federalist orientation.

The more federalist among the governments, however, felt that the Maastricht Treaty did not go far enough. With the decisive new monetary powers and the prospect of further enlargement, they wanted to make the Union more effective and democratic. By the time the Treaty entered into force, accession negotiations with Austria, Finland, and Sweden had already begun, and Cyprus, Malta, Norway, and Switzerland had lodged their applications. Norway negotiated an accession treaty but it was again rejected in a referendum; and the Swiss government withdrew its application after defeat in a referendum on the much looser European Economic Area. Negotiations with Cyprus and Malta were to begin in 1998 and 2001 at the same times as those with ten Central and East European states, following the European Council's decision that the latter could join when they fulfilled the economic and political conditions. But Austria, Finland, and Sweden acceded in 1995. So the Maastricht Treaty was followed in 1996 by another IGC, from which emerged the Amsterdam Treaty, signed in 1997 and in force in 1999.

The Amsterdam Treaty revisited a number of the Union's competences, including those relating to the two intergovernmental pillars. A new chapter on employment was added to the Community Treaty, reflecting concern about the unemployment that had persisted through the 1990s at a level around 10 per cent, together with fears that it might be aggravated if the European Central Bank were to pursue a tight money policy.

Among the institutions, the European Parliament gained most, with co-decision extended to include the majority of legislative decisions, and the right of approval over the appointment not only of the Commission as a whole, but before that, of its President. Since the President, once approved, was given the right to accept or reject the nominations for the other members of the Commission, the Parliament's power over the Commission was considerably enhanced. Its part in the process that led to the Commission's resignation in March 1999 and in the appointment of the new Commission demonstrated the significance of parliamentary control over the executive. The treaty also gave the Commission's President more power over the other Commissioners.

At the same time as adding these federal elements to the institutions, the Amsterdam Treaty reflected fears that the Union would not be able to meet the challenges ahead if new developments were to be inhibited by the unanimity procedure. This led to a procedure of 'enhanced cooperation', allowing a group of member states to proceed with a project in which a minority did not wish to participate, though at the time of writing the procedure has not yet been used. Six weeks before the meeting of the European Council in Amsterdam that reached agreement on the treaty, Tony Blair became Prime Minister following Labour's election victory. The new British government adopted the social chapter and, expressing a more favourable attitude towards the Union, accepted without demur such reforms as the increase in the Parliament's powers. But Britain, along with Denmark and Ireland, did opt out of the provision to abolish frontier controls, along with the partial transfer of the related cooperation in justice and home affairs to the Community pillar, even if the British government was later to cooperate quite energetically in that field. As regards external security, Europe's weak performance in former Yugoslavia had spurred demands for a stronger defence capacity; and Britain both accepted provision for this in the Amsterdam Treaty and then joined with France to initiate action along these lines.

Enlargement to 28, Constitutionalization, and Lisbon

Following their emergence from Soviet domination, ten Central and East European states obtained association with the Union, and then sought accession. They faced an enormous task of transforming their economies and polities from centralized communist control to the market economies and pluralist democracies that membership required. But by 1997 the Union judged that five of them had made enough progress to justify starting accession negotiations in the following year; and negotiations with another five opened in January 2000. By 2004, accession was completed for the Czech Republic, Estonia, Hungary, Latvia, Lithuania, Poland, Slovakia, and Slovenia, together with Cyprus and Malta; and Bulgaria and Romania joined in 2007. Turkey's candidature was also recognized; but the economic and political problems were such that negotiations were not opened until 2005 and look set to continue for many years yet, especially in light of opposition from several member states.

With such a formidable enlargement ahead, the question of deepening arose again. Reform of some policies was necessary, in particular for agriculture and the structural funds. The Commission's proposals for this, entitled *Agenda 2000*, were partially adopted, though further measures were required. As regards reform of the institutions, another IGC was convened in 2000, leading to the Nice Treaty which was signed in 2001 and in force in 2002.

The result was an inadequate response to the prospect of nearly doubling the number of member states. It introduced modest increases in the scope of qualified majority voting in the Council and of legislative co-decision with the Parliament, and some procedural improvements for the Court of Justice. It addressed the growth in the number of Commissioners accompanying enlargement by further enhancing the power of the President over the other Commissioners and taking some steps to limit their number. It also saw the 'solemn proclamation' of the Charter of Fundamental Rights, as a means of strengthening the Union's provisions in this field. But the weighting of votes in the Council and the number of MEPs for each state became the subject of unprincipled horse-trading, with an outcome that is not comprehensible to the vast majority of citizens. The German and Italian governments found the Treaty so unsatisfactory that they proposed a 'deeper and wider debate about the future of the Union'; and the European Council in December 2001, under Belgian presidency, decided to establish a Convention to make further proposals to an IGC in 2004.

The Laeken Declaration, named after the Brussels suburb where the European Council met, was cleverly crafted to secure unanimous agreement by including, in what amounted to terms of reference for the Convention, items aimed at the more intergovernmentalist as well as the more federalist members. So the Convention met in February 2002 with a very broad remit, and its 105 members covered a wide spectrum of political orientations, with two MPs from each of the then 27 member and candidate states plus Turkey as a forthcoming candidate, 16 MEPs, one representative of each government, two members of the European Commission, a President, and two Vice-Presidents.

The President of the Convention, former French President Valéry Giscard d'Estaing, steered a deft course between federalism and intergovernmentalism. The majority of its members, including MPs from member states, preferred a more federal than intergovernmental orientation; and Giscard satisfied them by favouring elements of federal reform within the Community pillar.

29

But the amended EU Treaty drafted by the Convention would not be unanimously accepted by the ensuing IGC if the federal elements intruded too far into the fields of common foreign and security policy, and macroeconomic policy. Nor would some of the representatives of heads of government in the Convention have accepted the consensus that Giscard sought as the outcome of its work; and Giscard himself may well have sympathized with this view. So he steered the Convention towards more intergovernmental proposals in those fields. In July 2003 it acclaimed a consensus on a draft Constitution. Its main thrust was towards more effective and democratic institutions, while also tidying up much of the existing Treaty provisions for common policies, and provided a basis for further development of a common defence. The IGC was convened in October 2003, agreed some amendments in an intergovernmental direction, and concluded a year later when all the member and acceding states signed the Treaty establishing a Constitution for Europe. Eighteen of them ratified the Treaty, but it was rejected by substantial majorities in French and Dutch referendums in 2005.

It can be read as a mark of the resilience of the integration process that despite the publics of two founding members being unwilling to approve a more explicitly constitutional grounding for the Union, there was still a desire to persist on the part of national governments, albeit after a 'period of reflection'. The continuing mismatch between elite and popular engagement with the EU since Maastricht was doubtless exacerbated by the former's unwillingness to generate debate about what is too often dismissed as remote or complex. Certainly, the revival of the large majority of the Constitutional Treaty's contents with a brief IGC in 2007 and a ratification that almost completely sidestepped ratification referendums did little to endear the Union to the public. This was borne out by a 'no' vote in Ireland (the one country to hold such a referendum) and legal challenges in Germany and the Czech Republic, all of which meant that the final document, the Treaty of Lisbon, only entered into force in December 2009.

Despite being the end result of such a fundamental review of the Union's legal basis and of almost a decade's worth of debate, the Lisbon Treaty looks a lot like its predecessors. It retains the basic mix of intergovernmental and federal elements, keeps member states in a privileged position of decision-making, and keeps many competences where they were previously to be found. However, it does mark a new stage in the Union's development.

Most importantly, Lisbon ended the pillar system, pulling all of the remnants of the second and third pillars into the first, which was governed by the renamed Treaty on the Functioning of the European Union (TFEU). The Treaty on European Union (TEU) remained to provide a wider framework and legal personality for the Union, as well as space for the Charter of Fundamental Rights to gain legal status in underpinning the Union's activities. Voting in the Council was simplified, while the Parliament further extended its legislative power, with the Ordinary Legislative Procedure (OLP) applying to most activities, and with a final say on all areas of spending. The European Council acquired a permanent President to chair and represent it, replacing the rotating Presidency, which was now confined to the Council. The Treaty further consolidated external representation, by creating a High Representative for Foreign Affairs, who would be simultaneously a vice-president of the Commission and chair of the Foreign Affairs Council. Importantly, formal roles were given to national parliaments to challenge legislative proposals, and to European citizens to submit petitions for action by the Commission.

For many, the Lisbon Treaty represented the end of an era of constitutionalization in the Union's affairs. However, the rapid deterioration of the global economy from 2007, which was to come to take up much more of Europe's politicians' attentions in the years that followed, has highlighted the need for a continued debate. The initial financial crisis, triggered by a collapse in banks' solvency, affected European economies hard, breaking a long period of growth. To this was added from 2009 a sovereign-debt crisis, specific to the Eurozone.

We discuss this further in Chapter 4, but here we would note that despite the varied causes of the sovereign-debt crisis, these were all compounded by the incomplete nature of the Eurozone's integration. With the Union lacking the capacity to generate Eurozone-wide fiscal transfers or debt creation, global financial markets were able to force governments into repeated rounds of crisis management and intervention, most obviously with the case of Greece. The progress of the crisis was such that gradually more major interventions became necessary, until by 2010–11 a raft of proposals came to the fore. Some of these were legislative, but some required amendment of the Treaties. Concerns about the impact on the City of London led the British government to block an attempt to do this in December 2011, with the result that other member states simply produced an agreement on a Fiscal Compact in early 2012, sitting outside the Union but using its institutions.

With an uncertain economic outlook, the European Union appears to have weathered the crisis, with the danger of individual member states leaving the euro having receded. The accession of Croatia in mid-2013 has shown the continuing relevance of the Union in securing peace and stability, but what remains unclear is the impact both on the Union's governance and on popular attitudes to integration. These are questions to which we will return.

Chapter 3
How the EU is governed

The EU has major economic and environmental powers, and is increasingly active in foreign policy, defence, and internal security. How is this power used and controlled? How is the Union governed?

The answer, according to many intergovernmentalists, is through cooperation among the governments of member states: the other institutions are peripheral to the Council in which the governments are represented, and this fact will not go away. But while the Council is still the most powerful institution, federalists regard the Parliament, Commission, and Court of Justice not only as sufficiently independent of the states to have changed the nature of the relationships among them, but also as major actors in a process that may, and should, result in the Union becoming a federal polity.

The European Council and the Council

The Council consists of ministers representing the member states; and at the highest level there is the European Council of Heads of State or Government together with the President of the European Council and President of the European Commission. Heads of state are included in the title because several presidents

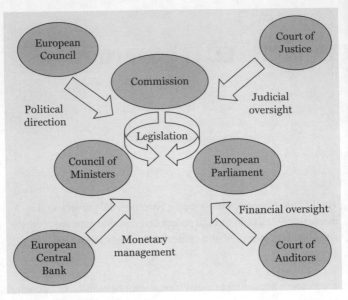

Chart 1 The Union's institutions

participate as well as their prime ministers, since they have some of the functions performed by heads of government elsewhere.

The European Council meets three or four times a year and takes decisions that require resolution or impulsion at that political level, sometimes because ministers have been unable to resolve an issue in the Council, sometimes because a package deal involving many subjects, such as a major amending treaty or a seven-year financial perspective, has to be assembled. The European Council also has to 'define general political guidelines'. Its rotating presidency is an important function, both for the management of current business and for launching new projects.

The President of the European Council is the closest that the Union has come to a national equivalent, representing the EU externally and providing a focus to the European Council's work.

Its first incumbent—former Belgian Prime Minister Herman Van Rompuy—has focused primarily on the managerial aspect of the post, helping to coordinate the response to the Eurozone crisis, and establishing a *modus vivendi* with the other institutions, most notably the Commission.

The meetings themselves are confined to two presidents (of the European Council and the Commission) and the 28 heads of state and government, and usually the Union's High Representative for Foreign Affairs. Outside the meeting room, they are surrounded by a vast media circus which presents the results to the citizens of different countries in radically different ways, with each leader seeking to make the best possible impression on their respective constituencies.

The 'Presidency Conclusions' are issued after each meeting, usually in a lengthy document, sometimes with bulky annexes.

7. European Council, 1979: facing different ways

The European Council itself initiates only a few of their decisions, and does not have time for thorough discussion of all that is put before it, especially when dealing with technical briefs, as in the Eurozone crisis. More typically, most of the detail and the 'political guidelines' emerge from the Union's institutions, working with the European Council's President.

The Council of the European Union (or Council of Ministers, as it is usually known) is a more complicated body. Which minister attends a given meeting depends on the subject. The Council meets in approximately ten forms, including an Economic and Financial Council (Ecofin), an Agriculture Council, a Foreign Affairs Council (under the chair of the High Representative), and a General Affairs Council comprising the foreign ministers, which is supposed to coordinate the work of the other Councils, but is in practice hard put to control Councils of ministers from powerful departments of state. Each Council is chaired by the representative of the state that is serving in turn for six months as President-in-Office.

Unlike the European Council, large numbers attend the meetings of the Council. Several officials as well as ministers or their representatives from each member state are present; and they are joined by the relevant Commissioners. Officials from the Commission also attend, as well as those from the Council Secretariat, which provides continuity from one presidency to the next and has become quite a powerful institution. Also unlike the European Council, much of the Council's work is legislative and some is executive.

After protracted pressure the Council now holds its legislative sessions in public, but its proceedings remain more like negotiations in a diplomatic conference than a debate in a normal democratic legislature.

The resemblance to an international negotiation was yet more pronounced before the mid-1980s when, with the launching of the single market programme, qualified majority voting (QMV) began

8. Council of Ministers: not a cosy conclave

to replace unanimity as the procedure for legislative decisions. Though the treaty stipulated that only texts proposed by the Commission could be enacted into law, the unanimity procedure had given each minister a veto with which to pressure the Commission into amending its proposal; and although the treaty provided for QMV on a range of subjects, the veto implicit in the Luxembourg 'compromise' extended its scope in practice to virtually the whole of legislation. The Committee of Permanent Representatives of the member states (called Coreper, after its French acronym) seeks common ground beforehand in the governments' reactions to the Commission's proposals; and given the difficulty of securing unanimity, it was thanks to the dedication of many of these officials that the Union was able to function at all. But measures identified by the Commission as being in the general interest and enjoying the support of a large majority were often reduced to a 'lowest common denominator', reached after long delay.

This contributed to the failure to make much progress towards the single market until the voting procedures were changed following the Single European Act. Up to then, single market measures had been passed at a rate of about one a month, barely enough to keep up with new developments in the economy, let alone complete the whole programme inside a quarter of a century. But the Single Act's provision for QMV on most of the single market legislation helped speed the rate to about one a week, putting the bulk of the laws in place by 1992.

The system for QMV has undergone several iterations. At present, there is a triple hurdle of a 67 per cent majority of states, a 62 per cent majority of population, and a 74 per cent majority of voting weights (i.e. 260 out of 352 votes, weighted roughly to size). This messy system came out of late-night bargaining at the Nice IGC and its complexities prompted the Convention and then the Lisbon Treaty to produce a simpler model. This model will apply from 2014, and requires 55 per cent of states and 65 per cent of population to reach the threshold: this decouples the system from the previous squabbles over voting weights, while protecting both large and small states from being structurally marginalized.

While QMV is designed to ensure that laws wanted by a substantial majority can be passed, the Council still tries to avoid overriding a minority of one government about something it regards as important. This is due partly to the need to treat minorities with care in a diverse polity, and that motive has an edge in the EU, where a disgruntled government could retaliate by bringing business to a halt on other matters still subject to unanimity. Partly it reflects the diplomatic culture which prevails in the Council. But unlike the Luxembourg 'compromise', votes are quite often taken, and proceedings take place in 'the shadow of the vote', so that ministers prefer to compromise than to run the risk that a vote will produce an outcome which is worse for them. Often the President, judging that a problem has been resolved, suggests that a consensus has been reached and, if there is no dissent, the Council accepts the text without a formal vote.

With the use of QMV for single market legislation, the Luxembourg veto began to fade away, so that QMV became the context for a wider range of decisions; and it was extended by the successive treaties to cover almost all fields of legislation. The remaining handful to which unanimity applies come under a variety of headings. These typically relate to structural issues, such as membership of the Union, enhanced cooperation, and citizenship, or to policy areas of particular sensitivity. Most notably for the daily operation of the Union, much of foreign policy has retained unanimity, as discussed in Chapter 8. Obviously, the greater the number of member states, the harder it becomes to reach unanimous agreement. So pressure has always existed to reduce the scope for the unanimity procedure and this has been a source of conflict between those with more, or less, federalist orientation. A similar argument arises about the Council's executive role.

Unlike a legislative body in most democracies, the Council exercises significant executive powers. Although the Commission is, as Monnet envisaged, the Union's principal executive body, the Treaty allows the Council to 'impose requirements' on the way in which the Commission implements the laws, or even to see to their implementation itself. This used to happen under a complex system known as 'comitology', where individual committees of member state officials supervised implementation of particular pieces of legislation. While some oversight was possible by the Commission and Parliament, the scope for obstruction and delay led to its partial replacement at Lisbon by a new 'delegated acts' process, which removes these committees for certain legislation, and the renaming of comitology as 'implementing acts'. However, this new system remains deeply opaque, not least because it is at the discretion of the legislators to decide which system to use. Certainly, the long-standing concerns about the transparency of this part of the legislative process will continue for many years yet.

The European Parliament

Members of the European Parliament (MEPs) are directly elected by citizens throughout the Union in June of every fifth year. There are 751 of them, distributed among the member states in proportions that favour the smaller states, though to a lesser degree than in the weighting of votes in the Council: ranging from 99 from Germany; 72 each from France, Italy, and the UK; and 50 each from Poland and Spain; down to 6 each from Cyprus, Estonia, Luxembourg, and Malta.

The political culture of the European Parliament differs radically from that of the Council. The meetings are open to the public; voting by simple majority is the routine; and the MEPs usually

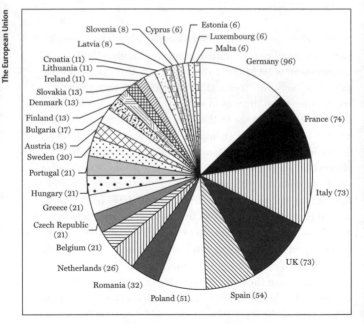

Chart 2 Number of MEPs from each state, 2014

vote by party group rather than by state. Three-quarters of the MEPs elected in June 2009 belonged to the mainstream party groups: 271 to the centre-right Christian Democrat and Conservative EPP (European People's Party) group; 189 to the centre-left PES (Party of European Socialists) group; and 85 to the ALDE (European Liberals, Democrats, and Reformists) group. The rest were evenly divided between smaller groups to the left, of which the most important were the Greens, and to the right, with a variety of eurosceptics of various ideological complexions.

While agreement has not yet been reached on a uniform electoral procedure, or 'principles common to all member states' as the Amsterdam Treaty more tolerantly put it, all the states now operate systems of proportional representation. The balance between the mainstream parties has otherwise been fairly stable, with neither the centre-right nor the centre-left able to command a majority alone. Hence broad coalitions across the centre are needed to ensure a majority for voting on legislation or the budget; and this is all the more necessary for amending or rejecting measures under the increasingly important co-decision procedure, where an absolute majority of 376 votes is required. The well-developed system of committees, each preparing the Parliament's positions and grilling the Commissioners in a field of the Union's activities, also tends to encourage consensual behaviour. But there has nonetheless been a sharper left–right division since the elections of 1999, when the centre-right became structurally larger than the centre-left, a pattern reinforced by enlargement.

Although the Parliament has performed well enough in using its now considerable powers over legislation and the budget, the voters' turnout has declined with each election, from 63.0 per cent in 1979 to 43 per cent in 2009. One reason is a general trend of declining turnouts in elections within member states. Another is a widespread decline in support for the Union. Yet another may be that the Parliament in particular has been exposed to critical and, particularly in Britain, downright hostile media comment,

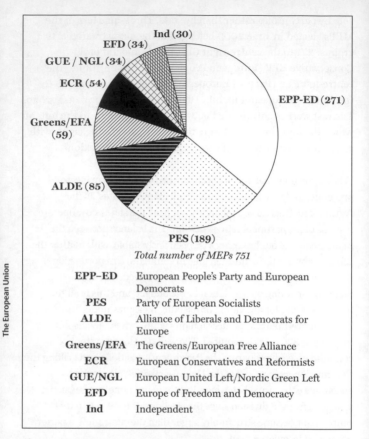

Chart 3 Party groups in the Parliament in 2012

fastening on matters such as the prolonged failure to establish an adequate system for controlling MEPs' expenses (largely the fault of MEPs themselves, though now in the process of being rectified), and the two costly buildings in Brussels and Strasbourg between which it commutes (entirely the fault of governments). Citizens may, moreover, not yet be aware of how much the Parliament's powers have grown over time.

The legislative role has developed from mere consultation at first, through the cooperation procedure initiated by the Single Act, to the co-decision introduced by the Maastricht Treaty and extended through to Lisbon to the point where it now applies to the large majority of legislation, under its new name of the Ordinary Legislative Procedure. In addition, Lisbon also gives the Parliament equal rights to agree the entire budget with the Council, allowing it to provide oversight into areas such as agriculture that had previously been shielded.

While the Parliament's share of power to determine the budget is an essential element of democratic control, its role in supervising how the money is spent has had the greatest impact. As well as its power of scrutiny over the Commission's administrative and financial activities, the Parliament has the right to grant 'discharge': to approve—or not—the Commission's implementation of the previous year's budget, on the basis of a report from the Court of Auditors. If not satisfied, the Parliament withholds discharge until the

9. **Elected representatives at work: European Parliament sitting**

Commission has undertaken to do what is required. Thus in 1998, after the Parliament had withheld discharge for the 1996 accounts and was not satisfied with the Commission's response, it appointed a high-level expert committee to investigate in more detail. They produced a devastating report on mismanagement and some cases of corruption; and the Commission, anticipating the Parliament's use of its power of dismissal, resigned in March 1999.

Having demonstrated its powers over both appointment and dismissal of the Commission, the Parliament is well placed to make clear to voters that it can in future use its influence to secure the appointment of a candidate for Commission President who reflects the results of European elections; and it has been suggested that a commitment by Parliament to do so could enhance voters' interest in the elections and thus strengthen the Union's representative democracy.

The Parliament shares power equally with the Council for most legislation and all of the budget; and it has proved much better able than the Council to control the Commission. So it can be said that the Parliament is more than halfway towards fulfilling the functions of enacting legislation and controlling the executive, which a house of the citizens in a federal legislature would perform. The Council for its part would be akin to a house of the states, save that the unanimity procedure still applies to some legislation, only its legislative sessions are held in public, and it has retained executive powers that ill accord with its legislative role.

The European Commission

While the Commission, as it stands today, is not the federal executive that Monnet envisaged, it is, with its right of 'legislative initiative' and its functions in executing Union policies and as 'watchdog of the Treaty', a great deal more than the secretariat of an international organization.

The Treaty of Rome gave the Commission the principal right of legislative initiative, that is, to propose the texts for laws to the Parliament and the Council. The aim was to ensure that the laws would be based more on a view of the general interest of the Community and its citizens than would result from initiatives of the member state governments, and that there would be more coherence in the legislative programme than they or the Councils with their various functional responsibilities could provide. Armed with this power, the Commission was in its early days often called the 'motor of the Community'. After it had been weakened by de Gaulle's assault in the 1960s, the balance of power swung towards the Council and, since its establishment in 1974, the European Council. But the Commission still performs the essential role of initiating both particular measures for the Council and Parliament to decide, and general policy packages in the European Council. Outstanding examples of the latter were the 'Delors package' of budgetary reform in 1992, and the *Agenda 2000* reforms of Community policies to prepare for the Eastern enlargement that were agreed in 1999.

The Commission has also been called the 'watchdog' because it has to ensure that the Union's treaty and laws are applied, notably by the member states. If it has evidence of an infringement, it has to issue a 'reasoned opinion' to the state in question. Should the latter fail to comply, the Commission can take it to the Court of Justice. This is what happened in 1999 when the French government refused to accept the Community's decision that British beef was by then safe to eat and its import should be allowed. The Court found in the UK's favour in late 2001, although it was not until 2006 that the other member states agreed to lift restrictions, and fines were imposed on France by the Commission in excess of €10 million. The Commission is also responsible for executing Union law and policy, though much of it is delegated to member state governments and other agencies.

In order to ensure that the Commission works in the general interest of the Union, the treaty requires that its independence of any outside interests be 'beyond doubt'; and the Commissioners, on taking up office, have to make a 'solemn undertaking' to that effect. Although the treaty provides for their nomination by 'common accord' among the governments, each government has in the past made its own nomination and this has been accepted by the others. But this can no longer be taken for granted, because the accord of the Commission's newly appointed President is now also required before the Parliament's approval of the Commission as a whole.

Until 2005 there were two Commissioners from each of the larger and one from each of the smaller states. But the impending enlargement caused concern that a larger Commission would be less effective, so the Nice Treaty limited the number of Commissioners, as from 2005, to one from each member state. Proposals for an even smaller number were stoutly resisted by smaller states, and the initial rejection of the Lisbon Treaty by Irish voters in 2008 resulted in agreement that the current system will remain.

Reducing the number of Commissioners to fewer than one per state is by no means the only way to secure effectiveness. The top tier of governments, such as the British Cabinet, usually has over 20 members, in some cases over 30; and this has worked because a prime minister has the power to control the other members. Treaties since Amsterdam have moved the Commission some way in that direction by giving the President the power not only to share in the decisions to nominate the other Commissioners, but also to exercise 'political guidance' over the Commissioners, to allocate and 'reshuffle' their responsibilities, to appoint Vice-Presidents, and to sack a Commissioner 'after obtaining the collective approval of the Commission'. The presence of the Union's High Representative for Foreign Policy as a Vice-President since Lisbon has also helped to provide management of policy coordination, both internally and externally.

10. The first meeting of the Commission with President José Manuel Barroso, 2004

In treaty terminology, the Commission is the whole body of Commissioners. In common usage, it also refers to the Commission's staff. But it is usually clear whether reference is being made to the Commissioners or the 25,000 employees; and despite loose talk of a bloated bureaucracy, this is fewer than the numbers employed by many local authorities.

Since QMV now applies to the bulk of legislation, the Commission's sole right of initiative has given it a strong position in the legislative process. The Council can amend the Commission's text, but only by unanimity, which here works in the Commission's favour instead of against it, for while the Commission normally prefers to accommodate governments' wishes, it is better placed to resist their pressure on points it regards as important.

The Commission has performed its legislative role well. But its performance as an executive has been heavily criticized. Much of the criticism has been unfair, where the execution is in fact

47

delegated to the member states. This is a good principle, which works well in Germany's federal system where the Länder administer most of the federal policies. But there the federal government has more power to ensure adequate performance from the Länder, whereas member states tend to resist the Commission's efforts to supervise them. The answer is surely not more direct administration by Brussels, but enough Commission staff to undertake the supervision and stronger powers to ensure proper implementation by the states.

The Commission has a good record in fields such as the administration of competition policy, where it was given the power to do the job itself and has done it well despite a shortage of officials. But there have been serious defects when it has been required to administer expenditure programmes without the staff who can do this properly, resulting in defects either in its own work or in that of consultants hired to do it, with sometimes bad and in a few cases fraudulent consequences. This stimulated not only the 1999 resignation, but also the ongoing reforms to the administration set out by Neil Kinnock in the early 2000s, aimed at improving recruitment, training, promotion, and audit practices.

Some have argued that the Commission is a European government. How far could this be an accurate description? Within the fields of Union competence, its right of legislative initiative resembles that of a government, and even exceeds it in so far as the Commission's is almost a sole right. But its use of the right is constrained by the Council, particularly where the unanimity procedure applies, though also by the use of QMV rather than a simple majority. The difference is, however, greater in comparison with Britain than with states that practise a consensual style of coalition government. The Commission's executive role is constrained by the Council and the difficulties of implementation but is otherwise not, in principle, far different from that of the

11. Rule of law: the Court of Justice sitting

German federal government, apart from the German
government's more effective means of enforcing proper
implementation by the Länder. A crucial distinction between
the Commission and a government is, indeed, that the
Commission does not control any physical means of
enforcement. It has moreover only a minor role in general
foreign policy, and very little in defence. Along with the
differences, however, there are significant similarities.

The Court of Justice

The rule of law has been key to the success of the European
Union. Increasingly, in its fields of competence, a framework of
law rather than relative power governs the relations between
member states and applies to their citizens. This establishes 'legal
certainty', which is prized by business people because it reduces a
major element of risk in their transactions. Politically, it has
helped to create the altogether new climate in which war between
the states is deemed to be unthinkable.

At the apex of the Union's legal system is the Court of Justice, which the treaties require to ensure that 'in the interpretation and application of the Treaties the law', taken here in a broad sense, 'is observed'.

There is one judge from each member state, appointed for a six-year term by common accord among the member states and whose independence is to be 'beyond doubt'. The Court itself judges cases such as those concerning the legality of Union acts, or actions by the Commission against a member state or by one member state against another, alleging failure to fulfil a treaty obligation. But the vast majority of cases involving Union law are those brought by individuals or companies against other such legal persons or governments; and these are tried in the member states' courts, coming before the Court of Justice only if one of those courts asks it to interpret a point of law.

The Court's most fundamental judgments, delivered in the 1960s, were based on its determination to ensure that the law was observed as the treaty required. The first, on the primacy of Union law, was designed to ensure its even application in all the member states; for the rule of law would progressively disintegrate should it be overridden by divergent national laws. The second, on direct effect, provided for individuals to claim their rights under the treaty directly in the states' courts. Then in 1979 a judgment on the 'Cassis de Dijon' case laid a cornerstone of the single market programme, with the principle of 'mutual recognition' of member states' standards for the safety of products, provided they were judged acceptable; and this radically reduced the need for detailed regulation at the Union level.

The Court has delivered some 9,000 judgments since its creation, and cases continue to come before it at a rate that makes it hard to reduce the delays of up to two years before judgments are reached. Two subsidiary courts were established to help deal with this problem: a 'General Court' (formerly the Court of First Instance), hearing almost all cases brought by individuals or legal persons, which relate mainly to intellectual property rights and to competition policy; and a 'Civil Service Tribunal', handling disputes between Union institutions and their staff. But this has stemmed, not turned, the tide of cases awaiting judgment.

While litigants can appeal from the lower Courts, there is no appeal beyond the Court of Justice, which is the final judicial authority on matters within Union competence. To enforce its judgments, however, it depends on the enforcement agencies of the member states. The fact that the large majority of judgments under Union law are made by the states' own courts has instilled the habit of enforcing it; and there has been no refusal to enforce the judgments of the Court itself, even if there have sometimes been quite long delays before member states have complied with judgments that went against them.

The Court's jurisdiction is still limited by the Treaties, especially in foreign policy. But within these limits, and apart from the almost total reliance on the member states' enforcement agencies, the Union's legal system has largely federal characteristics.

Subsidiarity and flexibility

In a speech delivered in Bruges in 1988, Mrs Thatcher famously evoked the spectre of a 'European super-state exercising a new dominance from Brussels'; and a 'slippery slope' leading towards a 'centralized super-state' has become a favourite metaphor for British eurosceptics. From a different starting point, German Länder have looked askance at proposals for Union competence in fields that belong to them in Germany's federal system. Indeed many federalists find the treaty objective of 'an ever closer union' too open-ended, and most support the principle of 'subsidiarity' as a guide to determine what the Union should do and what it should not do. That principle, which has both Calvinist and Catholic antecedents, requires bodies with responsibilities for larger areas to perform only the functions that those responsible for smaller areas within them cannot do for themselves. Following this principle, the treaty requires the Union to 'take action ... only if and insofar as the objective of the proposed action cannot be sufficiently achieved by the Member States', and can, 'by reason of its scale or effects, be better achieved by the Union'.

The Rome Treaty implicitly recognized this principle in distinguishing between two kinds of Union act: the Regulation, which is 'binding in its entirety' on all the member states; and the Directive, which is binding only 'as to the result to be achieved', leaving each state to choose the 'form and methods'. But this was a very partial application of the principle; and Directives were sometimes enacted in such detail as to leave little choice to the states. So the Maastricht Treaty defined subsidiarity and the Amsterdam Treaty laid down detailed procedures aiming to ensure that the principle would be practised by the Union institutions. The inclusion in the Lisbon Treaty of a list of which competences are exclusive to the Union, which are shared with member states, and which are supporting state action has further ensured that there are multiple safeguards against over-centralization.

There are of course disagreements about the fields in which integration is justified. These left their mark on the Maastricht Treaty, in the British opt-outs from the social chapter and the single currency, and those of Denmark on the single currency and defence. Since the treaty can be amended only by unanimity, the other governments had to accept the opting-out if these items were to be included in it; and this led to growing interest in the idea of 'flexibility', enabling those states wanting further integration in a given field to proceed within the Union institutions or, to put it the other way round, letting a minority opt out. One purpose was to circumvent the veto of individual member states, whose resistance to reforms might block that which most other governments regard as necessary, a concern heightened by enlargement to states that may prove unwilling or unable to proceed with further integration.

The concept of flexibility emerged in the Amsterdam Treaty under the heading of 'enhanced cooperation': a term preferred by federalists because it implied a deeper level of integration among a group of states, whereas eurosceptics tended to see flexibility as a way of loosening bonds in the Union as a whole. The Treaties now provide for enhanced cooperation within the Union provided that a number of conditions are met, including unanimous agreement that it be applied in any given case, that a minimum of eight states be involved at first, and that it remains open to any and all additional states.

Citizens

The concept of citizenship of the Union was introduced in the Maastricht Treaty, which provided that all nationals of the member states are also citizens of the Union; and the Amsterdam Treaty added that the two forms of citizenship are complementary. The Maastricht Treaty included a few new rights for the citizens, such as to move and reside freely throughout the Union subject to specified conditions, and to vote or stand in other member states in local and European, though not national, elections. This short list comes on top of specific rights already guaranteed by the treaties, such as protection for member states' citizens against discrimination based on nationality in fields of Union competence, and equal treatment for men and women in matters relating to employment. The Union's institutions are also required to respect fundamental rights, as guaranteed by the European Convention on Human Rights and Fundamental Freedoms. The Treaties affirm that the Union is 'founded on the principles of liberty, democracy, respect for human rights and fundamental freedoms, and the rule of law, principles which are common to the member states'; moreover it provides that, in the event of a 'serious and persistent breach' of these principles, a member state can be deprived of some of its rights under the treaty, including voting rights.

In response to concerns that the Union needs to do more to attract the support of its citizens, a Charter of Fundamental Rights was also drafted, in parallel with the Nice Treaty, by a Convention that set the precedent for the Convention which drafted the Constitutional Treaty. However, it was only with the Lisbon Treaty that the Charter gained legal force with regard to the actions of the Union itself. In addition, the Treaties provide for the Parliament to appoint an Ombudsman to investigate citizens' complaints about maladministration by Union institutions and report the results to Parliament and the institution concerned.

Apart from the question of rights, the system for governing the Union, with its complex mix of intergovernmental and federal elements, makes decision-making difficult and a satisfactory relationship between the institutions and the citizens hard to achieve. Yet unless the citizens develop sufficient support for the Union alongside that for their own states, the states' electorates could become a centrifugal force leading to disintegration; and the enlargement to 28, probably eventually over 30, states presents additional problems. There has been lively academic discussion on the need for a Union demos to sustain a Union democracy, which has encouraged scepticism regarding its possibility. The Union has, however, been able to benefit from its growing democratic elements such as the powers of the European Parliament, and it is unduly pessimistic to assume that the process cannot continue, along with the development of the Union as a whole. The solidarity among citizens remains far short of what would be necessary for a federal state. Substantial reform did come with the Lisbon Treaty, although this still leaves some questions unanswered.

Mostly importantly, Lisbon reaffirmed the need to balance the interests of the Union as a whole and those of member states. The removal of the pillar structure, the strengthening of the European Council with a permanent President, and the integration of foreign policy roles in the person of the High Representative offer the potential for a more coherent personality of the EU, although national governments have still sought to hold back common action. Similarly, while national parliaments now have powers to hold up a 'yellow card' to legislative proposals, those parliaments often lack sufficient surveillance mechanisms to make this truly efficient, just as the citizens' initiative, whereby a petition with one million signatures can trigger legislative action by the Commission, rests on a notion of a European public sphere that is more hope than substance at present. Perhaps just as significantly, Lisbon is the first treaty to provide for an explicit mechanism for a state to withdraw from membership.

The Eurozone crisis will be the next bridge for the Union to cross, especially if the discussions in late 2012 about new institutions to support a banking and economic union come to fruition. Whatever the outcome, it should remind us that the Union reflects the needs of its citizens, and these change over time, so it is only right that there remains an air of contingency over the form of its organization.

Chapter 4
Single market, single currency

While peace among the member states remained at the heart of
the Community's purpose, from the second half of the 1950s a
large common market became the focus for its action. The
strength of the US economy was a striking example of the success
of such a market; the Germans and the Dutch wanted liberal
trade; and the French accepted the common market in industrial
goods provided it was accompanied by the agricultural common
market that would favour their own exports.

The idea of a large common market had a dynamic that endured
through the subsequent decades, because it reflected the
growing reality of economic interdependence. As technologies
developed, and with them economies of scale, more and more
firms of all sizes needed access to a large, secure market; and for
the health of the economy and the benefit of the consumers, the
market had to be big enough to provide scope for competition,
even among the largest firms. So as the European economies
developed, the EEC's original project, centred on abolition of
tariffs in a customs union, was succeeded in the 1980s by the
single market programme, then in the 1990s by the single
currency.

There were both economic and political motives for each of the three projects: the benefits of economic rationality; and the consolidation of the Community system as a framework for peaceful relations among the member states. Economics and politics were also both involved in the substance and outcomes of the projects, because the integration of modern economies requires a framework of law, and hence common political and judicial institutions. Nor would success in either the economic or the political field alone have been enough to sustain the Community. There had to be success in both, which the customs union and the single market each achieved. It was also a combination of economic and political motives that secured the launch of the single currency, though not yet the participation of all member states.

The single market

Tariffs and import quotas were, in the 1950s, still the principal barriers to trade. The international process of reducing them began under American leadership in the Gatt (General Agreement on Tariffs and Trade). But the member states of the Community wanted to do more. The result was the EEC's customs union, abolishing tariff and quota barriers to their mutual trade, and creating a common external tariff.

Customs union, competition policy

Tariffs and quotas on trade between the member states were removed by stages between 1958 and 1968. Industry responded positively and trade across the frontiers grew rapidly, more than doubling during the decade.

While tariffs and quotas were the main distortions impeding trade, they were not the only ones. The Community was also given powers to forbid restrictive practices and abuse of dominant positions in the private sector. The treaty gave the task to the Commission, without intervention by member state governments;

and in 1989 the Commission was also given the power to control mergers and acquisitions big enough to pose a threat to competition in the Community. Armed with these powers, the Commission has done much to discourage anti-competitive behaviour and has been seen as the toughest cartel-buster in the world. Thus in 2008, it fined Saint Gobain €895 million for illegal market sharing in car glass. Because of the volume of work, the Commission sought to return some of these responsibilities to the member states' competition authorities. There was pressure from business interests to prevent this, because they find it convenient to have the Commission as a 'one-stop shop', but some degree of decentralization did occur with the creation of the European Competition Network, in which the Commission and national authorities share information and coordinate investigations.

Unfair competition can also take the form of subsidies given by a member state government to a firm or sector (in the EU jargon 'state aids'), enabling it to undercut efficient competitors and undermine their viability. The Commission has been given the power to forbid such subsidies. But it has been harder to control governments than firms. The Commission has been able to enforce some difficult decisions on reluctant governments; but especially in the 1970s, after it had been weakened by de Gaulle and with the economies hard hit by recession, it could do little to stem the rising tide of subsidies.

Along with the subsidies, non-tariff barriers proliferated in those years, becoming the main obstacle to trade between member states. One reason was technological progress, generating complex regulations differing from one state to another. More important was pressure for protection from those who were suffering from the prevailing 'stagflation'. The European economy was indeed in bad shape, vividly evoked by the term 'eurosclerosis'. A way out was sought; and the Commission, together with leading business interests, persuaded governments that a programme to complete the Community's internal market was required.

Programme to complete the single market by 1992

With the success of the internal tariff disarmament in the 1960s in mind, some business leaders and members of the Commission's staff worked on the idea of a programme to remove the non-tariff barriers. When Delors became the Commission's President in 1985, he fastened onto this idea as the only major initiative that would be supported by the governments of all the member states: the majority because of its economic merits and the political aim of 'relaunching the Community' after two rather stagnant decades; Mrs Thatcher because of economic liberalization alone. But she did the Community the service of nominating the highly capable Lord Cockfield, who had been trade minister in her Cabinet, as a Commissioner to work with Delors on the project.

Delors and Cockfield put the project to the European Council in June 1985. Whereas the programme for eliminating tariffs in the 1960s could be specified in the treaty in the form of percentage reductions, the removal of non-tariff barriers required a vast programme of Community legislation. Frontier formalities and discrimination resulting from standards and regulations, from public purchasing, and from anomalies in indirect taxation all had to be tackled. The Commission published a White Paper specifying that some 300 measures would have to be enacted and proposing a timetable for completing the programme within eight years. This was approved by the European Council and incorporated in the Single European Act, making completion of the programme by the end of 1992 a treaty obligation.

The removal of non-tariff barriers was already implicit in the Rome Treaty, which prohibited 'all measures having equivalent effect' to import quotas. But because the practice of voting by unanimity had impeded the legislative process, the Single Act provided for qualified majority voting on most of the measures needed to complete the programme. The Commission also reduced the legislative burden by building on the principle of mutual recognition that the Court had established by its judgment in the Cassis de Dijon case, and by delegating decisions on much of the detail to existing standards institutes. Nevertheless, the single market remained a huge enterprise, surely one of the greatest programmes of legislation liberalizing trade in the history of the world.

It was an outstanding success. The latter half of the 1980s was a period of economic regeneration in the Community. While one cannot be sure how much of that was due to the single market programme, economic research has given it at least some of the credit. The programme certainly contributed to the recovery by generating positive views of business prospects as well as stimulating trade, together with structural reform exemplified by a spate of cross-border mergers. The industrially less-developed states—Greece, Portugal, and, at that time, Ireland and Spain—fearing they would be damaged by stronger competitors, had secured a doubling of the structural funds to help them adjust; and they too, assisted by this and by the expanding Community economy, benefited from the programme.

Politically, the single market enjoyed a remarkable degree of approval across the spectrum from federalists to eurosceptics. It has been a classic example of a purpose that is, as the treaty's article on subsidiarity puts it, 'by reason of scale...better achieved by the Community'. The legislative framework has guaranteed producers a very large market and given the consumer a reasonable assurance of competitive behaviour among them. The Commission, Council, and Parliament were strengthened by their successful output, comprising a large part of the vast 'acquis', as the jargon puts it, of Union legislation; and the role of the Court was accordingly enhanced.

The programme was largely completed, but significant gaps still remain. The most notable area of difficulties has been in the field of liberalization of services. Despite representing over two-thirds of EU GDP, there is little cross-border provision, not least because

of fears in old member states about cheap labour coming from
Central and Eastern Europe. This was seen most vividly in the
French referendum campaign on the Constitutional Treaty in
2005, when the 'Bolkestein Directive', which aimed to liberalize
services within the Union, became a symbol of social dumping,
and the 'Polish plumber' an object of intense political concern.
When the Bolkestein Directive was agreed in 2006, it had
undergone much modification, weakening its impact.

The single currency

A monetary union requires that money in all its forms can move
freely across the frontiers between member states and that
changes of exchange rates between them are abolished. The single
market programme went far to fulfil the first requirement and the
Exchange Rate Mechanism prepared the ground for the second.

The Exchange Rate Mechanism (ERM) was established in 1979,
after the abortive attempt to move to monetary union in the
1970s. It required the central banks to intervene in the currency
markets to keep fluctuations of their mutual exchange rates within
narrow bands; and by the end of the 1980s it had, with the
German Bundesbank as anchor, achieved a strong record of
monetary stability. Here again, Britain stood aside at the start,
only to join in 1990, at too high a rate and without the experience
of the preceding decade of cooperation. In September 1992,
currency turmoil forced the pound out of the ERM on what
became known as Black Wednesday, making monetary integration
a traumatic subject for many British politicians. The ERM had the
opposite effect in other member states, with the benefits of
exchange-rate stability flowing to economic operators, and in turn
allowed for more reinvestment in production and new
employment, particularly important in a single market.

Almost all governments supported the single currency project,
on political grounds even more than economic ones. The most

powerful commitment was in France, where a tradition of support for exchange-rate stability was bolstered by the desire to share in the control of a European central bank and thus recover some of the monetary autonomy that had in practice been lost to the Bundesbank. Other member states, apart from Denmark and the UK, accepted such arguments, especially in the context of a newly unified Germany. For Germany, however, while the political motive for accepting the single currency as a French condition of unification was decisive, there were still reservations about replacing the Deutschmark, with its well-earned strength and stability, by an unproven currency. However, the possibility of building a similar system across the Union was clearly an important motivating factor for an export-driven economy such as Germany's; if other states would accept the logic of macroeconomic coordination alongside the currency itself, then this would ultimately serve Germany's interests.

The aim of economic and monetary union

The Maastricht Treaty, in providing for economic and monetary union (Emu), established the European Central Bank (ECB) to be, like the Bundesbank, completely independent. The ECB and the central banks of the member states are together called the European System of Central Banks (ESCB). The six members of the ECB's Executive Board, together with the governors of the other central banks, comprise the Governing Council of the ECB; and none of these banks, nor any member of their decision-making organs, is to take instructions from any other body. The 'primary objective' of the ESCB is 'to maintain price stability' though, subject to that overriding requirement, it is also to support the Union's 'general economic policies'. The ECB has the sole right to authorize the issue of notes, and to approve the quantity of coins issued by the states' mints. In response to German preference, the single currency was named the euro, rather than the French-sounding ecu.

In order to ensure that only states which had achieved monetary stability should participate in the euro, five 'convergence criteria' were established, regarding rates of inflation and of interest, ceilings for budget deficits and for total public debt, and stability of exchange rates. Budget deficits, for example, were not to exceed 3 per cent of GDP and public debt was to be limited to 60 per cent of GDP, unless it was 'sufficiently diminishing' and approaching the limit 'at a satisfactory pace'. Only states that had satisfied the criteria were to be allowed to participate; and once again, stages and a timetable were fixed, in order to give at least a minimum number of states the time to do so. Others were to have 'derogations' until they satisfied the criteria, while the British and Danes negotiated opt-outs allowing them to remain outside unless they should choose to join.

In the first stage all were to accept the ERM, as Britain had briefly done before being ejected by market forces. In the second stage they were to make enough progress to satisfy the convergence criteria. The third stage began in January 1999 with the 'irrevocable fixing of exchange rates' among the participating states, leading in 2002 to the introduction of the new euro notes and coins which replaced the participants' currencies entirely.

During the mid-1990s, there had been much concern about which countries would be able to achieve the convergence criteria, partly for economic reasons (as with the case of Italy) and partly owing to more political factors relating to the degree of strictness with which the criteria would be interpreted by the EU. In the event, an economic upswing and strong political pressure allowed 11 of the 13 states to join in 1999, with only Greece being specifically excluded (although it was given the green light one year later), while the Swedish government had decided that membership was not politically viable and had asked not to move forward without its approval.

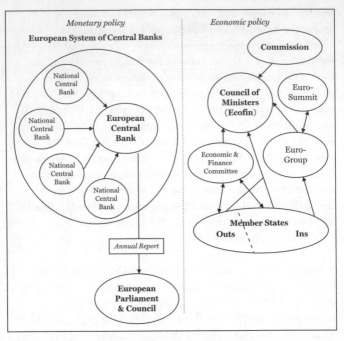

Chart 4 Institutions of economic and monetary policy

Thus by 2002 the very large majority of member states were Eurozone participants and the issue of relations with those outside became a matter of some concern, because of the binary model of economic policy coordination it required. At least formally, all member states are committed to eventual membership, but in practice the lack of popular support in the UK, Denmark, and Sweden, especially in the wake of the Eurozone crisis, means that the situation is likely to persist for the foreseeable future. In the UK, the Labour government parked the issue in 1999 with conditions relating to structural convergence, sufficient flexibility in Eurozone economies, and the impact on various economic markers; all are suitably vague in their

12. The euro: notes and coins

formulation, allowing any future government to make a decision on the basis of political factors. This was particularly important given the cross-party agreement that any decision would be made after a popular referendum.

The ambivalence of these three member states has been mirrored to a certain extent by newer members. While Slovenia, Malta, Cyprus, Slovakia, and Estonia have all joined the Eurozone, a number of other states have reined in some of their initial drive towards participation. Here the factors relate more to the economic flexibility that retaining a national currency allows, rather than any particular sense of the currency as a strong symbol of national identity. Moreover, all new member states are legally bound to introduce the euro as soon as possible, not having the opt-outs of the UK and Denmark.

A currency in crisis?

If the euro was initially acclaimed as the realization of a new stage in European integration, then recent years have exposed the flipside of this, with the euro as the crucible of political commitment to the Union. The extended period of economic growth in the 2000s perhaps lulled some into thinking that the asymmetrical design of Emu was not a problem, but the double blows of the financial crisis from 2007 and the sovereign-debt crisis a couple of years later were certain to raise them up into matters of acute concern.

The roots of the financial crisis lay in the deregulation of financial markets in the early 2000s and the subsequent ballooning of many global economies. The sudden collapse of many key market actors in 2007, as the scale and extent of exposure to bad debt became clear, resulted in a worldwide seizing-up of credit. This in turn made banks unwilling or unable to make loans to businesses, forcing governments to turn to classical Keynesian interventions to return liquidity to markets.

In and of itself, this would have been manageable within Emu as it existed, since macroeconomic policy and bank regulation were still in national hands. However, from 2009 financial markets turned their attention away from banks to governments and, more particularly, their debts. In particular, markets became increasingly concerned that member states of the Eurozone were holding excessive amounts of sovereign (i.e. government) debt, to the extent that this potentially compromised their ability either to service that debt or to maintain the solvency of national banking systems.

Eurozone membership certainly played a key role in this, as states that had previously had weaker fiscal management were able to benefit from the perceived extension of German rectitude across the Eurozone when issuing new debt, which could be sold at much lower rates than before. This encouraged a relaxing of fiscal management by those states, after their earlier efforts to meet the entry requirements to the single currency: the Stability and Growth Pact (SGP) that had been introduced in the Amsterdam Treaty was a belated attempt to maintain the stricter regime. However, its regular flouting in the mid-2000s by most member states (including Germany and France) meant that it was a dead letter and that it was only the generally favourable macroeconomic climate that made it possible to sustain the situation.

From 2010 onwards, Eurozone leaders engaged in a series of emergency measures to try and regain the initiative. This included the creation in May 2010 of the European Financial Stability Facility (EFSF), with access to some €750 billion to provide extensive support to Eurozone members. The EFSF has been the vehicle for the bailouts provided to Ireland, Portugal, and Greece, the latter twice to date. These bailouts have been accompanied by requirements to implement assorted supply-side reforms, in order to promote conditions for more sustainable long-term growth. The increased willingness of the ECB, under its President Mario Draghi, to provide cheap loans to banks and a backstop to sovereign debt since 2012 has also acted as a means of easing pressure, albeit temporarily.

If the EFSF and ECB have provided a short-term source of relief, then there has also been an effort to put in place long-term mechanisms in order to ensure that the crisis cannot occur again. This progressed in three main stages. First, there was a reform of the SGP with the so-called 'Sixpack' of legislation passed in 2011 to allow for stricter enforcement of the SGP's provisions on excessive deficits: coupled to the Euro-Plus Pact and its supply-side reforms of Eurozone economies, this set out a framework for action. However, the limitations of this approach helped to push the EU and Eurozone into a second phase, from late 2011, when the European Fiscal Compact was agreed.

The Compact, or the Treaty on Stability, Coordination, and Governance in the Economic and Monetary Union (TSCG) as it is formally known, lies outside the EU's legal framework but can use the Union's institutions. This curious arrangement resulted from the unwillingness of the British government at the December 2011 European Council to agree to a Treaty revision in the more usual fashion, having asked for protection for the City of London as a global financial centre and been rebuffed. This blockage—together with the Czech government—meant that both Eurozone members and most other EU members had to take a more intergovernmental route to the Compact's main objective of legal requirements for national budgets to be in balance. The Compact provides for stronger monitoring and enforcement mechanisms at the European level, including the possibility of legal action before the Court. In so doing, the Eurozone has sought to give markets increased confidence in the long-term sustainability of the currency area.

In support of the Compact, there was also agreement to move the EFSF to a more permanent basis, with the creation in 2012 of the European Stability Mechanism (ESM). The Mechanism replaces the EFSF and provides a much more extensive set of financial reserves to support struggling Eurozone economies. In contrast to the Compact, it sits firmly within the Union's system of enhanced cooperation, applying to all Eurozone members.

However, even with the rapid negotiation and agreement on the Fiscal Compact, 2012 saw renewed pressure, which in turn has forced governments and the Commission back to the drawing board. In this current phase, the debate is now about integration beyond coordination, potentially through the unification of banking regulation by 2014 and then into something akin to a full economic union. This latter development would imply integrated national budgets and oversight by the Commission, as well as fiscal union with the creation of jointly held sovereign debt. However, all of these proposals remain to be fleshed out and properly negotiated, given the qualitative leap that they would represent.

The consequence of all of these developments has been to move Emu into a new phase of its existence, where the pressures of very negative market forces have exposed the limitations of the asymmetric design laid out in the Maastricht Treaty. Accordingly, Eurozone members have been forced to reinforce their commitment to the euro, and strengthen a number of key aspects of their economic and fiscal integration.

However, Emu does not lead inevitably to a federal state. A federal state extends its central powers over the use of force; and this does not follow from the adoption of the euro. The argument about defence integration, which is addressed later, is a different one. As regards strengthening the institutions and making them more democratic, that is already desirable, with or without the single currency; and it will become essential if the Union is to be capable of satisfying its citizens' needs and avoid the risk of disintegration.

Chapter 5

Agriculture, regions, budget: conflicts over who gets what

The single market is a positive-sum game. Because it enhances productivity in the economy, there is benefit for most people, whether they take it in the form of consuming more or working less. But alongside the majority who gain, there will be some who lose, or at least fear they will lose, from the opening of markets to new competition; and these may demand compensation for agreeing to participate in the new arrangements. Such compensation usually has implications for the Union budget and looks like a zero-sum game, which can lead to conflict between those who pay and those who receive, even if the package of compensation and competition, taken together, benefits both parties. The first major example was the inclusion of agriculture in the EEC's common market.

Agriculture

The opening of the Community's market to trade in manufactures was, when the EEC was founded, a relatively simple matter of eliminating tariffs and quotas by stages. But tariff and quota disarmament was only a small part of the problem of creating an agricultural common market. All

European countries managed their agricultural markets with complex devices such as subsidies and price supports to ensure adequate incomes for farmers and security of food supplies. So a common market for agriculture would have to be a complicated managed market for the Community, to replace those of the member states. It would have been simpler to confine the common market to industry. But the French feared the prospect of German industrial competition and, having a competitive agricultural sector, insisted that the Community market be opened to agriculture too.

The result was the common agricultural policy, with prices of the main products supported at levels decided by the Council of agriculture ministers, through variable levies on imports from outside the Community and purchase of surplus production into storage at the support level. Farmers' incomes were bolstered by high prices paid by the consumer, together with subsidies from the Community's taxpayers to finance the surpluses that the high prices evoked. While this was tenable in the Community's early years, once the UK became a member new tensions arose. The British model of free trade had meant that prices had been much lower, so membership of the common agricultural policy (CAP) meant a triple blow of higher prices for food, high levels of British contributions to the budget, because of import levies on foodstuffs, and low receipts from the budget, because of the small size of its agricultural sector.

This state of affairs was to trigger a five-year battle after Mrs Thatcher became Prime Minister in 1979, blocking much other Community business as her method of what she called 'getting our money back'. Matters came to a head in 1984, when the accumulation of stocks such as 'butter mountains' and 'wine lakes' had cost so much that the Community needed to raise the ceiling for its revenue from taxation; and this required unanimous agreement by the member states. So a deal was done, with agreement on a higher ceiling for tax resources allocated to the Community and an annual rebate for Britain at around two-thirds of its net contribution. At the same time a step was taken to reform the CAP, but only a modest step, because attention had been focused on the questions of the rebate and the tax resources.

Stages of reform

The CAP lumbered on, accumulating further costly surpluses, until 1988 when the money ran out again. This time the financial interests of member states prevailed. With the division of the Council into functional formations, the decisions of the Council of agriculture ministers on prices of farm products had determined the level of the bulk of Community expenditure, over which the Council of finance ministers had little say. Since the resulting bill had to be paid out of the Community's tax resources, the agriculture ministers were in effect deciding on the rate of tax paid by the citizens to the Community. Financial control had to be established and the European Council agreed in 1988 on a package of measures, proposed by Delors, which introduced a 'financial perspective' setting limits for the main headings of the Community's expenditure during the five years 1988–92. The growth of spending on agriculture was restricted to less than three-quarters of the rate of growth of the total.

While this took some of the heat out of the conflict over money, a serious reform of the CAP was still required. By 1992 the Commissioner responsible for agriculture was Ray MacSharry, a former Irish minister. He grasped the nettle and, outmanœuvring the opposing interests, secured a cut of 15 per cent in the support price for beef and nearly one-third for cereals. The current levels of expenditure were not reduced, because farmers were compensated with income supports, including 'set-aside' payments for leaving cultivated land to lie fallow. But the measures removed the expansionary dynamic from the CAP and prepared the ground for further reform.

The cost of the CAP remained a heavy burden for the Community, with half the budget going to support a sector that employs less than 5 per cent of the working population, much of it for a small minority of the bigger and richer farmers. By the end of the 1990s, moreover, the twin pressures of enlargement to the East and negotiations in the newly established World Trade Organization (WTO) were forcing the EU into a more structural reform process. New member states, with their large agricultural sectors, were set to drive up costs very significantly, while the need to secure agreement in WTO trade liberalization negotiations was placing increasing pressure on reductions in levels of agricultural support. Consequently, the Union agreed substantial cuts for some products in 1999, as part of wider budgetary negotiations, as well as introducing the notion of a multifunctional CAP, i.e. one that extends into the social and environmental dimensions that surround farming. This recasting of the CAP as a 'rural' policy—confirmed by the 2008 'health check'—was an important step in helping to unblock the reforms that some states, notably France, had put on hold.

This became much more apparent at the 'Mid-Term Review' of the 1999 agreement in 2003, with what had initially been considered a simple review of the changes producing reforms as important as those of MacSharry a decade previously. Again the amount of price support was cut, but the main revolution was the shift to direct support for farmers. Until then, the CAP had used price support mechanisms to pay farmers, thus providing a strong incentive to over-produce: hence the wine lakes and butter mountains of the 1980s. The new Single Farm Payment (SFP) introduced in 2006 separates (or 'decouples' in the jargon) payment from production: instead farmers are paid to look after their land, regardless of whether they choose to farm it or not.

The breaking of the old model of price support was perhaps inevitable in the face of the pressures that the CAP had faced over the previous 40 years. The combination of enlargement, WTO

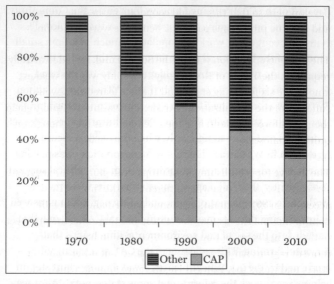

Chart 5 Share of budget spent on CAP, 1970–2010 (*percentage of total budget*)

negotiations, rising environmental concerns, and public health scares ultimately proved too powerful to resist. What is still not clear is how the CAP will develop in the medium term: the new member states are natural supporters of a substantial CAP that pays their farmers well, while the notion of a more multifunctional approach to rural development has become a much more dominant discourse within the institutions. Either way, it would appear that the CAP is set to experience yet more change.

Cohesion and structural funds

The 'cohesion policy', the other big item of expenditure in the Union's budget, has been a happier experience than the CAP. It stems from fears in member states with weaker economies that they would lose in free competition within the Union. When the customs union, the single market, and the single currency were established, funds were provided to assist their economic development so that they would cooperate in these new ventures and become prosperous partners: hence the word 'cohesion'.

The first such provision was for the Social Fund, included at Italy's request in the Treaty of Rome. Italy's economy was the weakest among the six founding states and Italians feared they would suffer from the liberalization of trade. They wanted a fund to help their workforce to adapt; and their demand was met, though on quite a small scale.

The motive for establishing the European Regional Development Fund (ERDF) was somewhat different. By the time of British accession in 1973, Britain's economic performance had fallen behind those of the six founder states; and there was the prospect of the big net contribution for the CAP. Britain had its share and more of regions with economic difficulties, but other member states had theirs too. Edward Heath's government, which had negotiated British accession, had the sound idea that a fund for regional assistance would both respond to a general interest and be of particular value to Britain, not only assisting its regional development but also reducing its net contribution to the Community budget. While the initial impact of the fund was weak, it has developed into the main source of financing for cohesion.

The third of what became known as the 'structural funds', in order to underline that their aim was not just to redistribute money but rather to improve economic performance in the weaker parts of the Union's economy, is the European Agricultural Fund for Rural Development (formerly the 'Guidance Section' of the European Agricultural Guidance and Guarantee Fund (EAGGF)), which helps farmers carry out structural change. But the three structural funds, though at first small, grew steadily and were available to respond to the demand for a major expansion in the 1980s when the Community was enlarged to the south.

Enlargement and structural funds

When Spain, Portugal, and Greece joined the Community, their average incomes were far below those of the other member states save Ireland, which before its phenomenal growth in the 1990s was at a similar level. These four countries, led by Spain, demanded a major increase in the structural funds, and their ability to block agreement on the passage of the single market legislation meant the Single Act contained an article on 'economic and social cohesion'; Delors proposed that the budget for the structural funds be doubled in the financial perspective for 1988–92; and this was accepted by the European Council.

A similar problem emerged when it was decided to embark on Emu, with the same four states seeking a similar expansion of the structural funds. This time Delors secured an increase of two-fifths in the allocation for the period 1993–9; and the Maastricht Treaty provided for the establishment of the Cohesion Fund, to support projects in the fields of the environment and transport infrastructure. By 2000 the budget for the funds was €32 billion.

The four states for which the expansion of the structural funds was originally designed have performed for the most part well, the current Eurozone crisis notwithstanding. Spain has been very successful, though less outstandingly so than Ireland; Portugal had to check its initially rapid growth with a stabilization programme. The Greek case has been much more complex, with the finance available through the funds being counteracted by more structural macroeconomic problems. While it is not possible to say how much of this generally good result can be attributed to the structural funds, the contributions of 2–4 per cent of GDP certainly eased the path.

Although the objectives of the structural funds had been focused on help for regions where development was 'lagging behind', it has

Box 2 Structural funds and objectives

Since the early 1970s, the Union has developed its regional policies around a set of funds and objectives. These were reformed in 1999 and again in 2006.

The structural funds now comprise:
- the European Regional Development Fund (ERDF)—deals with regional development and economic change;
- the European Social Fund (ESF)—concerned with re-training workers;
- Cohesion Fund—aimed at poorer member states, this fund develops projects in the environment and infrastructure.

For the 2007–13 planning period, spending has been focused on three key objectives:
- Convergence (areas with GDP per head less than 75 per cent of the EU average)—roughly €45 billion per year is spent helping regions with a population of 154 million;
- Regional Competitiveness & Employment (helping areas to make structural adjustments to meet new economic situations and to adjust labour forces)—€9 billion per year goes to regions with a population of 314 million;
- European Territorial Cooperation (developing cross-border links between member states)—over €1 billion per year to help regions with 182 million people living in them.

always been a feature of cohesion policy that all member states get something back out of the budget. Partly this is a reflection of the diversity of the states, but it is also driven by the unanimity required to conclude budgetary planning negotiations. This posed a particular problem with the enlargement to the East, since under the policy that prevailed in the late 1990s, new member states stood to receive very large amounts of funding, while existing member states stood to lose out.

The response to this was, as with the CAP, to engage in some fairly drastic reforms. The growth in funding for cohesion was capped in the financial perspective agreed at Berlin in 1999, since richer member states were not prepared to foot the bill, while simultaneously it was decided that most of the existing funding should be ring-fenced for existing members, regardless of new members' objective needs. Coupled with the Commission's pronouncement that transfers to any member state would be capped to the equivalent of 4 per cent of GDP, on the grounds that this was the most any country would usefully absorb, when enlargement did come in 2004 its impacts on the budget were relatively attenuated. Despite average incomes in new member states being typically half to two-thirds the EU average, they receive only one-third of cohesion funding. While this proportion is more than the one-fifth of the EU's population that they represent, it is still less than would seem to be necessary to help them move reasonably fast towards comparable standards of economic development. The negotiations for the 2014–20 period are likely to result in a larger share of funding going to these poorer states, albeit with everyone still getting something to take home.

Thus while the cohesion policy has, unlike the CAP, been relatively harmonious, it is important to recognize the limitations that member states have placed on maximizing its benefit for the Union as a whole. This posture has also increasingly affected the budget as a whole.

The budget

With agriculture and cohesion now accounting for about 40 per cent each of EU expenditure, the two together, with their powerfully redistributive effects, account for the bulk of spending. The cost of administration in the Union's institutions comes to less than 6 per cent of the total, and the remainder goes to finance a range of internal and external policies. A major item of redistribution outside the budget is the rebate to reduce the British net contribution, which amounted in 2010 to €3.5 billion and is paid direct to Britain by the other member states.

The total expenditure in the budget for 2012 was €147.2 billion, or 1.12 per cent of Union GNP. This has to remain below 1.24 per cent of GNP unless that ceiling is increased by a decision ratified by all the member states; and the financial perspective for the years 2007–13 keeps spending below 1 per cent of GNP in each year.

'Own resources'

Unlike international organizations that depend on contributions from their member states, the EU's revenue from taxes is a legal requirement under the treaty, subject, like other treaty obligations, to the authority of the Court of Justice. This is to prevent member states from holding the Union to ransom by withholding contributions. The consequences of such behaviour are demonstrated by the financial state of the United Nations, weakened for many years by the refusal of Congress to sanction payment of the due US contribution—ironically enough, since the

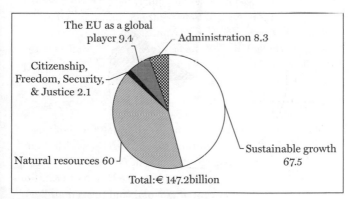

The EU as a global player 9.4
Administration 8.3
Citizenship, Freedom, Security, & Justice 2.1
Natural resources 60
Sustainable growth 67.5
Total:€ 147.2billion

Chart 6 Breakdown of budget expenditure, 2012 (€ billion)

failure of American states to pay their due contributions in the 1780s under the Articles of Confederation was a powerful argument in favour of the US federal constitution. The same argument influenced the EC's founding fathers to make the payment of tax revenue to the Community a legal obligation.

The EU has no physical means of enforcement should a member state not hand over the money. But the rule of law has been of sufficient value to the member states to be respected by them.

Initially the EEC's tax revenue, called in the treaty 'own resources' to underline the point that they belong to the Community not the states, comprised the takings from customs duties and agricultural import levies. But these were not enough to pay for the CAP, and the Community was allocated a share of value-added tax at a rate of 1 per cent of the value of the goods and services on which VAT is levied.

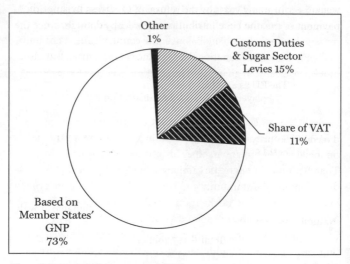

Chart 7 Sources of revenue, 2011 (%)

A major objection to these indirect taxes was that they bear hard on the poorer states and citizens, making them pay a higher proportion of incomes than the richer. So in 1988 a fourth resource was introduced, in the form of a small percentage of the gross national product of each member state. This is roughly proportional to incomes and by 2012 accounted for almost three-quarters of the EU's revenue. But the total outcome of the revenue system is still regressive.

Net contributions

As mentioned above, it was Mrs Thatcher who first coined the phrase 'our money back', although the British had, since their accession in 1973, been constantly seeking redress for what they could claim to be an 'unacceptable situation' resulting from a financial regulation adopted just before they joined. Previously, the fact that some member states got more out of the budget than others was taken simply as part of the package of membership. In particular, the Germans, who had willingly accepted for many years their role as the largest net contributor, did so because they recognized that the benefits of membership could not be measured simply by a bank balance: the country gained not only in deeply desired international acceptance and security, but also, more prosaically, in giving German exporters access to large new markets.

Nonetheless, since the 1980s, and particularly since the mid-1990s, member states have become much more aware of the financial costs of membership. This was driven in part by Mrs Thatcher and her energetic campaign, but also by the development of Community and Union policies. The large growth of cohesion spending further reinforced the north–south divide between net contributors and recipients, while the growth in importance of the fourth resource effectively renationalized budgetary receipts. In addition, existing member states were concerned about the budgetary implications of enlargement.

Box 3 States' net budgetary payments or receipts
(*percentage of GNI, 2010, minus sign net payments*)

Net contributors		Net recipients	
Belgium	−0.41	Cyprus	0.06
Germany	−0.36	Spain	0.39
Sweden	−0.34	Ireland	0.64
United Kingdom	−0.33	Malta	0.91
Netherlands	−0.31	Romania	1.03
Italy	−0.30	Slovenia	1.19
France	−0.26	Czech Republic	1.53
Denmark	−0.26	Portugal	1.57
Austria	−0.24	Greece	1.61
Finland	−0.16	Slovakia	2.07
Luxembourg	−0.14	Poland	2.47
		Bulgaria	2.55
		Hungary	2.94
		Latvia	3.67
		Estonia	4.86
		Lithuania	5.03

Source: European Commission, *EU Budget 2010 Financial Report*, 2011

Coupled to Germany's increasing reluctance to foot the bills, reform became increasingly inevitable.

In 1999, the Berlin European Council agreed to reduce the amount that Germany, the Netherlands, Austria, and Sweden, the then net contributors, paid towards the British rebate. That rebate remained a bone of contention, since the original case of over-contributions and under-receipts was less and less compelling, but successive British governments were loath to give up an income stream of several billion pounds a year. Nonetheless, as enlargement became a reality, the British did demonstrate some willingness to reduce the level of their rebate, in order to minimize the burden on the new member states, agreeing in 2005 to take a reduction of the rebate of €10.5 billion between 2007 and 2013, equivalent to roughly one-quarter of the total value. This was intended to help the British case for a more general review of spending policies and budgetary procedure, although there was very little to show for it and the issue has been a source of contention in the negotiations of the 2014–20 financial perspectives.

Of more concern is the lack of growth in the EU's overall budget. Since 1999, there has been a reduction in the ceiling of expenditure as a percentage of GNP. Even with the growth of that GNP over time, the budget remains very small in comparison with member state governments' budgets. This is a somewhat unfair comparison, since the EU does not have to spend on social security, defence, health, education, or any of the major items that we typically associate with public activities. However, the size of the budget does constrain what the Union can do, for example in promoting cohesion and balanced development across all its member states. While it does appear to have weathered the transition to an enlarged membership, it is evident that further reforms will be needed if the Union is to remain a relevant actor, both internally and in the wider world.

Chapter 6
Social policy, environmental policy

The EU has been given some of its powers, such as those to establish the single market, because its size offers advantages that are beyond the reach of the individual member states. Other powers are designed to prevent member states from damaging each other. The environment is one field in which powers have been given to that end, with general agreement that it is desirable. Another is social policy, where there has been sharp disagreement as to how far EU intervention is required.

Social policy

The term 'social policy' has a narrower meaning in EU parlance than it generally has in Britain. It does not refer to the range of policies, including health, housing, and social services, with which the welfare state is concerned. The pattern of such services differs from country to country, reflecting their political and social cultures; and it is widely accepted that the cross-border effects of the differences are not sufficient to justify intervention by the Union. In the Treaty and EU jargon, however, social policy concerns matters relating to employment, where there are also wide variations from country to country. But since conditions of employment touch more closely on the single market, there has been pressure to harmonize member states' policies in order to prevent employees in states with higher standards suffering as a result of competition from those with lower standards.

The first such example was the article on equal pay in the Treaty of Rome. France was ahead of other founder states in having legislated that women be paid equally with men for equal work. In order to keep sectors that employed a high proportion of women competitive, France demanded that its partners introduce equal pay too. With the general movement towards gender equality, this was to become one of the most popular European laws. By the time of the Amsterdam Treaty, there was ready agreement to extend the principle from equal pay to equal opportunities and equal treatment in all matters relating to employment.

The Single European Act extended the scope of social policy in two directions: providing for legislation on health and safety at work and for the encouragement of dialogue between representatives of management and labour at European level. While Mrs Thatcher had fought hard against the influence of 'corporatist' relationships in Britain, she doubtless reckoned that such dialogue at European level would not be of much consequence; and the case against undercutting standards of health and safety was generally agreed. So although Community social policy was to become one of Thatcher's bêtes noires, she accepted these provisions of the Single Act as part of the package that included the single market programme.

In 1989 Delors, who saw higher standards of social legislation as being, for workers, a necessary counterpart to the single market, proposed a Social Charter that was approved by all but one in the European Council. Thatcher dissented. Although she accepted some of its provisions, such as free movement for workers and the right to join (or not) a trade union, she contested others, such as a right for workers to participate in companies' decision-taking, as well as maximum working hours—which, much to the British

85

government's disgust, were subsequently enacted by a qualified majority vote under the treaty article on health and safety at work. Major followed her example when he secured Britain's opt-out from the provisions on social policy in the Maastricht Treaty, which therefore appeared in a protocol that applied to all the other member states. It was only after Labour's election victory in 1997 that there was unanimous agreement to convert the protocol into a social chapter in the Amsterdam Treaty; and it was accompanied by a new chapter aimed at achieving 'a high level of employment and of social protection'. But Britain has continued to promote the cause of flexible labour markets, an objective that was taken up in the 2000 Lisbon Agenda and its successor, the 2010 'Europe 2020', which brought together social policy with employment policy in a combination that was much more oriented to the use of economic growth to provide for social well-being.

Flexibility or regulation in labour markets

Britain has emphasized deregulation and flexibility in its approach to the EU, on the grounds that it will make the European economy more competitive and increase employment. While labour markets are not the only sector of the economy in which deregulation is advocated, they are seen as among the most important.

While this British approach has been called 'Anglo-Saxon' because of similarities with American economic philosophy, an alternative became known as the 'Rhineland' approach, with Germany the leading example. There the emphasis in labour markets has been on solidarity and social protection rather than flexibility. Much of the regulation to achieve this has been negotiated between employers and unions, called in Germany the 'social partners'. This has reflected a culture of consensus in civil society in reaction against the ways of the preceding totalitarian dictatorship; and it has built on long-standing traditions of solidarity, such as the acceptance of responsibility in the private sector for the high standards of technical training. The results have included the outstanding economic success of the post-war decades and the continuing strength of German exports. But although the burden of integrating the eastern Länder into the German economy is one cause of the less successful performance in the 1990s, Germany is also criticized for reluctance to introduce more flexibility into the labour market and to reform industrial and financial organization and the tax system, in response to current developments in the global economy.

The Rhine also flows through the Netherlands; and the Dutch too have a highly consensual economic and political system.

Box 4 Employment policy

The Amsterdam Treaty introduced a new section on employment in response to concern about the high level of unemployment in the EU. Its main purpose is to encourage cooperation among the member states with respect to their employment policies.

The member states provide annual reports on their employment policies to the Council and Commission, which draw up a report for the European Council. Guidelines are then issued to the states to be taken into account in their employment policies; and the Council can make recommendations to governments. The Council, in co-decision with the Parliament, may decide to spend money from the budget to encourage exchanges of information and best practices, provide comparative analysis and advice, promote innovative approaches, and fund pilot projects.

This has raised the profile of employment policy in the Union but it remains to be seen how much effect it has on governments' policies.

Faced with critical economic problems in the 1980s, they began a process of reform which led to what is called the 'Polder model', introducing market-oriented reforms into what remains a consensual system; and they achieved lower unemployment, higher efficiency, and a good all-round economic performance. Scandinavians have much in common with this approach.

The French, while stressing social protection, rely more on government leadership and regulation; and they too, despite criticism that they were slow to reform, performed well through the 1990s on most measures save their high rate of unemployment. But unemployment has remained particularly high among young people; and the economy became gradually less successful. So President Nicolas Sarkozy began to lighten the regulatory burden.

It is often forgotten that the British, for more than three decades after World War Two, had an economy that was highly regulated by both collective bargaining and government intervention. It was in reaction against this that the reforms of the Thatcher period moved Britain sharply towards the Anglo-Saxon model. While the intention of Blair's 'third way' was to prevent such oscillation by occupying a centre ground in between, much of the emphasis on economic flexibility and his government's enterprise-friendly orientation derived from his predecessors' reforms, as well as from an older British tradition of economic liberalism.

The improved British economic performance since the 1990s has helped to give credibility to the Anglo-Saxon approach, as has the dynamism of the Irish economy. But most important was the sustained success of the American economy, with its low unemployment and high growth, from which the conclusion could be drawn that flexibility suits the current stage of technological development. While the degree of laissez-faire in the American approach to social policy is resisted, a certain consensus may be emerging in the EU that methods such as bench-marking and peer pressure are more suitable than social legislation for reducing unemployment, as well as for some measures to create a dynamic and competitive economy. While there is still a strong constituency within several large member states for an interventionist approach to such questions, the rise of globalization, the need to maintain competitiveness, and, more recently, the Eurozone crisis have moved the debate within the Union towards the British viewpoint. Whether and how far supply-side reform will take place remain to be seen.

Environmental policy

Polluted air and water cannot be prevented from moving out of one state and causing damage in another. So there is an interest in common standards to control the pollution at its source. The same applies to the environmental effects of goods traded in the single market. The Single European Act provided for a Community environmental policy to deal with these problems. It also affirmed that the EC's objective was to 'preserve, protect and improve the quality of the environment'.

Several hundred environmental measures have been enacted, responding to a wide range of environmental concerns: air and water pollution; waste disposal; noise limits for aircraft and motor vehicles; wildlife habitats; quality standards for drinking and bathing water. In 1988 a law was passed to reduce the incidence of acid rain, cutting emissions of sulphur dioxide and nitrogen oxides by 58 per cent by stages over the following 15 years. Standards of protection against dangerous chemicals were demanded following the accession of the environmentally conscious Swedes in 1995; and the highly complex REACH directive for guaranteeing standards throughout the Union was finally passed in 2006. While Union legislation had always allowed member states to set their own higher standards in other matters, Scandinavian pressure led to an article in the Amsterdam Treaty allowing states to have higher standards for traded products too, provided they can persuade the Commission that these are not protectionist devices; and by 2004, the 'polluter pays' principle became Union law. The focus on environmental policy came at a time when Europeans were rapidly becoming greener, so it became one of the Union's most popular policies, as the provision for equal pay had done before; and like policy for gender equality, it too was strengthened by the Amsterdam Treaty, which stipulated that 'environmental protection requirements' must be integrated into other Union policies 'with a view to promoting sustainable development'.

The Sixth Environmental Action Programme, which the Council and Parliament approved in 2002, contained a ten-year framework for promoting sustainable development, in the fields of climate change, nature and biodiversity, environment and health, and natural resources and waste. Later in that year the Union played a leading role in the World Summit on Sustainable Development in South Africa. Sustainable development strategy has subsequently been a priority, with climate change the most prominent element, gaining an explicit mention in the Lisbon Treaty.

The Union's action with respect to climate change has had a powerful impact, both internally and in the wider world. The EU signed the Kyoto Protocol in 1998, with its target of cutting emissions of greenhouse gases by 2012 to 8 per cent below the 1990 level. The Council then, in a somewhat fraught process, allocated quotas to the member states for their emissions, on a proposal from the Commission after consultation with each state, to a total estimated to keep the Union's emissions within the target. The emissions are carefully monitored and there are penalties for non-compliance. In 2005 the Union, in order to provide flexibility in the control of emissions, introduced its Emissions Trading Scheme (ETS), which allocates the rights among more than 5,000 of the Union's major industrial polluters, allowing those that emit less than their quotas to sell the unused rights to those that use more, and thus creating a 'carbon market' which determines the cost of carbon within the Union. Since the rights were evidently issued too generously initially, the ETS will now auction credits, helping to raise the carbon price high enough to discourage excessive use. This is particularly important since the European Council decided in 2006, following the best scientific advice, that the Union must achieve a 60 per cent cut by 2050, in line with the global target deemed necessary to avoid potentially catastrophic change; and since, as is shown in Chapter 10, the Union is leading the world in this field, it needs to maintain its own credibility.

Chapter 7
'An area of freedom, security, and justice'

Ernest Bevin, the great Foreign Secretary in the first post-war Labour government, said that the aim of his foreign policy 'really was...to grapple with the whole problem of passports and visas', so that he could 'go down to Victoria Station', where trains departed for the Continent, 'get a railway ticket, and go where the Hell I liked without a passport or anything else'. The old trade unionist retained his vision of the brotherhood of man. But the foreign minister found himself defending the sovereignty of states; and he rejected the idea of British membership of the emergent Community, which was eventually to make the realization of his vision feasible.

Already in 1958 the Rome Treaty included 'persons', along with goods, services, and capital, in the four freedoms of movement across the frontiers between the member states. For 'persons' this was limited to the right to cross them for purposes of work. A quarter of a century later, the Single European Act defined the internal market as 'an area without internal frontiers'. Mrs Thatcher's government held that these words implied no change, because they were qualified by the addition 'in accordance with the Treaty', which in relevant respects still stood. But governments of the more federalist states intended to take the words literally: to abolish controls at their mutual borders and thus make movement across them free for all.

This idea was given legal expression in the Schengen Agreements of 1985 and 1990, Schengen being the small town in Luxembourg, symbolically alongside the frontiers with both France and Germany, where these three states, together with Belgium and the Netherlands, signed the agreements. The number of signatories has since grown until what has often been called Schengenland has been signed up to by all the EU states save Britain and Ireland, as well as Efta members.

Schengen had two main aims. The first concerned border controls: to eliminate those internal to Schengenland; establish controls round its external frontier; and set rules to deal with asylum, immigration, and the movement or residence of other countries' nationals within the area. The second was to cooperate in combating crime.

Cross-border criminal activity grows for reasons similar to those that drive cross-border economic activity: advancing technology, particularly in transport and communications. As with trade, cross-border cooperation is needed if the rule of law is to keep abreast of it. With the intense relationship engendered by their economic integration, the member states have a special need for such cooperation. A first step was taken in 1974 with the 'Trevi' agreement to exchange information about terrorism; and the ministers and officials involved soon found it useful to include other forms of crime. This was a precursor of Schengen, which forged closer cooperation among law enforcement agencies of the states that were ready to go further together, and which has led to an extensive 'acquis' of legal texts, applying to the very large majority of EU member states.

Maastricht's third pillar

Cross-border aspects of crime and the movement of people affect all member states, not just those of Schengenland. It was agreed that the Maastricht Treaty should provide for cooperation in these fields. Terrorism, drugs, fraud, and 'other serious forms of crime' were listed in the Treaty, along with external border controls, asylum, immigration, and movement across the internal borders by nationals from states outside the Union. The member states' judicial, administrative, police, and customs authorities were to cooperate in order to deal with them.

Some states, such as Germany, wanted this to be done within the Community institutions, with the Commission, Court, and Parliament as well as the Council playing their normal parts. Others such as Britain, defending their sovereignty, wanted to exclude as far as possible the institutions other than the Council. The upshot was the new 'third pillar' for Cooperation in Justice and Home Affairs (CJHA), set up alongside the Community 'first pillar'. The institutions for the CJHA were intergovernmental, with the unanimity procedure in the Council, only consultative roles for the Parliament and Commission, and none at all for the Court. The policy instruments were to be joint positions and actions determined by the Council, and conventions ratified by all the member states. One of the conventions was to establish the new policing body, Europol.

Not surprisingly, given the requirement of unanimous agreement among the then 15 governments before a decision could be taken, there had not been much progress by the time the Amsterdam Treaty was negotiated. No convention had yet entered into force and action in other respects was slow. But concern about cross-border crime and illegal immigration continued to grow; and the Eastern enlargement, expected to bring new problems, was approaching. So most member states wanted a stronger system.

Amsterdam's project

The Amsterdam Treaty affirmed the intention to establish what it rather grandly called 'an area of freedom, security, and justice' (AFSJ). This essentially meant that various third-pillar elements moved into the first pillar, under the Union's institutional control, most notably by the Parliament and the Court. Coupled to a new cycle of five-yearly programmes from 1999, and with the gradual adoption of the Charter of Fundamental Rights, AFSJ developed considerable momentum.

Lisbon brought further substantive change. The collapsing of the pillars has brought police and judicial cooperation into the Ordinary Legislative Procedure, albeit with some transitional arrangements and with member states allowed a limited right of initiative. While the Charter is now legally binding, several states, including the UK, have special provisions and opt-outs, reflecting the continued sensitivity of the policy field.

While conditions in the Union are, in a general sense, notably free, secure, and just when compared with almost all other parts of the world, the words are used in the treaty in a more specific sense: freedom refers to free movement across internal borders; security, to protection against cross-border crime; and justice, mainly to judicial cooperation in civil as well as criminal matters. It still remains to be seen whether it was wise to appropriate words that have such wide and noble significance for such particular ends. The answer may depend on how far and how soon they are achieved.

As regards *freedom* of movement, almost all the Schengen acquis has already been transferred into the Union. Thus the right of people to move freely throughout Schengenland is guaranteed by the institutions, though some member states have had to restore border checks temporarily in order to deal with influxes from other member states of non-EU nationals with false visas. The external border controls are not yet satisfactory. Nor is the common policy on immigration and asylum complete. Nor will there be freedom of movement without border checks throughout the Union while Britain, Denmark, and Ireland retain their controls. Determined to keep its border controls, Britain opted out of the Amsterdam Treaty's provisions on freedom of movement; and Ireland, enjoying open frontiers with the UK, had to do the same. But both have the right to opt into specific measures, provided the other governments agree unanimously in each case. The British government has said it intends eventually to participate fully in the Schengen acquis, apart from the aspects relating to border controls, while Denmark, which had signed up to the Schengen Agreements, has opted out of their transfer into the Union.

As regards *security*, the fight against cross-border crime remains primarily intergovernmental, albeit with extending influence of the Commission. With activity addressing trafficking in persons, offences against children, corruption, money-laundering, forging money, and 'cyber-crime', there has been significant activity. Europol has made a useful contribution, though it could not become fully operational until its convention was fully ratified by all member states in July 1999, over five years after the Maastricht Treaty had provided for it. Likewise, Frontex, established in 2005 to coordinate border guards, had a slow start, but now deploys teams to several of the Union's key frontiers.

However, it is in the field of counter-terrorism that most significant progress has been made. After the September 2001 attacks on the US, the Union quickly pushed to develop its own abilities to act. A European arrest warrant that had been in limbo for several years was agreed in 2002, alongside an action plan that targets aspects of the prevention and prosecution of terrorist acts, as well as coordinating responses by member states. Linked to this was the decision to create a high-level European Police College and a body called Eurojust, bringing together member states' prosecutors, magistrates, and police officers to cooperate in criminal investigation and prosecution.

In the narrow definition of *justice* as judicial cooperation, some specific steps have been taken for member states to assist each other in cross-border problems relating to the recognition and enforcement of judgments, though not much has been done about the rights of victims of crime. The path chosen by the Union has been one of mutual recognition, rather than harmonization; but there has been agreement on several joint policies, most notably the European arrest warrant, which address some of the problems of cross-border crime.

In a broader definition of the word, distributive justice has been an issue in this field since Germany, with a much larger number of asylum-seekers than other member states, wanted measures to share the cost. This resulted in the creation of a European asylum policy that has coordinated national policies and allowed for an improved management of the significant population flows in the post-Cold War world.

In a yet broader sense of justice, the Union has responded to criticism that it had emphasized restrictions on immigration and asylum at the expense of concern about the treatment of the human beings involved. In the face of widespread public backlash against these people, the Amsterdam Treaty provided for measures to safeguard their rights, together with action more generally to combat racism and xenophobia. Coupling these measures to the Charter on Fundamental Rights, the Union has now articulated a fairly substantial human rights protection programme, although the degree to which it can enforce this remains moot.

What's in the name?

Freedom of movement within Schengenland is an almost complete reality. If Bevin were able to go to the Gare du Nord or the Gare de Lyon today, he could buy a ticket and go without a passport wherever he liked within Schengenland, though not, unfortunately, to Victoria Station.

While Lisbon has brought much clarity to the organization of this policy field, it is far from certain that this goes far enough to tackle the various challenges. The persisting divisions between member states and the Union, as well as the differential memberships of the EU and Schengenland, result in confused lines of control, limited scope for action, and a system that few members of the public either know or understand. In many ways, the area of freedom, security, and justice is a classic example of the Union's wider problem: it is a potentially useful means for tackling problems that are beyond the scope of individual member states, but it is hampered by the political compromises, abstruse jargon, and occasionally counter-intuitive policies that result from trying to bring together such a large number of actors without adequate institutional reform.

Chapter 8
A great civilian power...
and more, or less?

The main motives for creating the Community were peace between France, Germany, and the other member states, and prosperity for their citizens. But while their mutual relationship was particularly intense, relations with their neighbours and with countries further afield were also very important; and the logic of subsidiarity, that the Community should have responsibility for what it can do better than the member states acting separately, began to be applied to external as well as internal affairs.

The Community's external relations were, in line with its powers, originally concentrated in the economic field. But there were from the outset also political aims. For Germany, bordering on the Soviet bloc and with East Germany under Soviet control, the priority was solidarity in resistance to Soviet pressure. The French had a broader vision of the Community as a power in the world. Relations with the United States were a central element: for Monnet, in the form of a partnership between the Community and the US; for de Gaulle, to defy American hegemony. Monnet's view was widely shared and the Community came to be seen as a potential 'great civilian power'.

Many in France went beyond this, envisaging a Europe that could challenge American dominance in the field of defence. In other countries this view was generally resisted. But cooperation in foreign policy evolved to the point where the Union gave it the name 'Common Foreign and Security Policy'; and Britain, which had long been adamantly opposed to common action by the EU on defence, in 1999 joined France in initiating a modest EU defence capacity. This is still a minor, though increasingly significant, element in the Union's external relations. The Union's external economic policies remain much more important.

Meanwhile, the world has been becoming a more dangerous place, with sources of instability such as climate change, environmental degradation, cross-border crime, poverty, consequent mass migration, and terrorism, alongside the military forms of insecurity. The relative simplicity of the confrontation between the United States and the Soviet Union has been replaced by American supremacy, and with the perspective of an emergent multipolar world in which the US is in the process of being joined by China and, probably later, India as giant powers, while Russia along with other, rising powers must also be taken into account; and the balance of bipolar economic power, with the predominance of the US and the EU, is being rapidly transformed, likewise with the BRIC economies of Brazil, Russia, India, and China, into a multipolar world economy. This is the world in which the EU has to find its place; and as the impact of the Iraq War of 2003 and the gridlocked Doha Round of trade negotiations have demonstrated, it is no simple task.

Europeans have generally reached a stage in their history, and particularly in the experience of living peaceably together in the EU, when they greatly value security and predictability in the relations among states, hence favour the creation of a secure multilateral system in the world. While the Union's military capabilities play a growing part in functions such as peacekeeping, its external economic, aid, and environmental policies, together with its experience in developing peaceful relations among states, have a major potential for contributing to both its own security and prosperity, and those in the wider world. In this perspective, much can be learned from the Union's experience so far. So we examine in this chapter why and how its structures for dealing with the rest of the world have been established; in Chapter 9, how it has come to be enlarged from 15 states in Western Europe to include most other European states; and in Chapter 10 how its policies for dealing with the rest of the world have been developed.

External economic relations

The Rome Treaty gave the Community its common external tariff as an instrument for trade policy, called in the jargon 'common commercial policy'. This was not a foregone conclusion. Some wanted the member states to keep their existing tariffs, below the average in Germany and Benelux, higher in France and Italy. But the French insisted on the common tariff, partly because they feared competition from cheap imports seeping through the low-tariff states, but partly also because they wanted the Community to have an instrument with which it could start to become a force in world affairs.

This has remained a persistent French theme. It was one of the motives for the drive towards the single currency, challenging the hegemony of the dollar; and it has continued with the effort to build a European defence capacity, for which the term 'Europe puissance' has been coined, contrasted with a mere European 'space' preoccupied with business affairs. Neither those French who were highly protectionist, nor the British who at that time criticized the common tariff as a protectionist device, envisaged that it would in fact be the trigger for the Kennedy Round of tariff cuts, which was the first step towards the Community's role as the foremost promoter of world trade liberalization, and thus also towards demonstrating the power of a common instrument of external policy.

That power has been shown in the field of agriculture too, with much less fortunate results. The system of import levies and export subsidies has been used in a highly protectionist way, to the detriment of the Community's consumers and international trade relations, including its own industrial exports. But the external trade policy, taken as a whole, has been of considerable benefit both to its citizens and to international trade.

External trade relations are conducted effectively by the Union institutions. Policies are decided and trade agreements approved by the Council under the procedure of qualified majority; negotiations are conducted by the Commission within the policy mandate thus decided, and in consultation with a special committee appointed by the Council; and the Court has jurisdiction on points of law. Parliaments do not usually play much part in relation to trade negotiations, apart from formally approving the results. But the Treaties did not even provide for consultation of the European Parliament about matters of trade policy, though it is accorded the right to give or withhold its assent over treaties of association and, more importantly, of accession, although the Parliament does play a significant part in external relations more generally.

When the Rome Treaty was drafted, trade in goods was all-important; trade in services was of little account, and was not mentioned in the chapter on the common commercial policy. But services now comprise about one-third of all world trade. Yet despite the success of the normal Union system as it applies to the trade in goods, trade in services has remained subject to more intergovernmental procedures. While the momentum of successful negotiations on trade in goods has carried the Union through a series of trade rounds, these procedures could still weaken its capacity to negotiate effectively on services. So the Nice Treaty applied qualified majority voting to trade in all services save in the fields of culture, audio-visual services, education, health and social services, and some transport services.

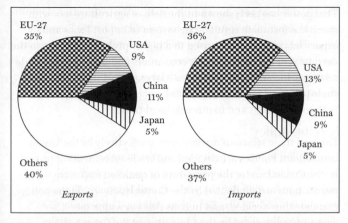

Chart 8 Shares of world trade of EU, US, China, Japan, and others, 2010

Development aid has also become a major instrument of the Union's external policy, initiated, likewise on French insistence, with the Rome Treaty's provision for a fund for the then colonies of member states. This has since burgeoned so that the Union provides aid for countries throughout the less-developed parts of the world. Thus the EU, together with its member states, has become by far the world's largest source of aid; and within Europe the Union's instruments of trade and aid policy, along with the prospect of membership, have been a major external influence favouring the successful transformation of the new member states from Central and Eastern Europe. It was indeed fortunate that France insisted on the original grant of instruments for the Community's external policy.

The environment too, and climate change in particular, has become a major field for international negotiation; and though the Union's external policy remains subject to a somewhat more intergovernmental procedure than its trade policy, the EU has nonetheless, as we shall see in Chapter 10, had a decisive impact on negotiations to counter global warming and destruction of the ozone layer.

103

The EU does not yet play a similar part in the international monetary system, despite the potential offered by the Eurozone crisis. The institutional arrangements for conducting an external monetary policy are not at present strong enough to enable it to exert its potential weight, although the ECB has clearly become an important player in policy debates.

Foreign policy

Cooperation in foreign policy among the member states was introduced in 1970 as an element of deepening along with the widening to include Britain, Ireland, and Denmark. The name given to this activity was European Political Cooperation (EPC): the word 'political' being used by ministries of foreign affairs, distinguishing what they saw as 'high politics' from such matters as economics, evidently regarded as low. But the Community's external economic policies were already a great deal more important than anything the EPC was to achieve during the following years, particularly as France, in the early years after de Gaulle, insisted that the EPC be kept not only intergovernmental but also rigorously separate from the Community.

The EPC did achieve an important early result when the member states got human rights placed on the agenda of the Conference on Security and Cooperation in Europe. The Soviet Union accepted the text that was finally adopted, which though nobody then thought it of much consequence, in the event gave support to the agitation that contributed to the dissolution of the Soviet bloc. More generally, the member states' diplomats developed ways of working together that were to produce many joint positions on a wide range of subjects, both in relations with other states and in the United Nations. By 1985 France was ready to accept that the EPC should come closer to the Community and it was included in the Single European Act.

The next formal development of foreign policy cooperation was its incorporation in the Maastricht Treaty alongside the Community, as the 'second pillar' of the EU. The prospect of German unification had alarmed the French, who feared that the larger Germany might downgrade the Franco-German partnership and pursue an autonomous Eastern policy. Just as they promoted the single currency to anchor Germany in the Community, so they wanted a common foreign policy to limit German autonomy in relations with the East; the Germans, far from opposing this, saw it as part of the design for a Europe united on federal lines; and both President Mitterrand and Chancellor Kohl saw a common foreign policy together with the single currency as cementing permanent peace in Europe. So they proposed the IGC on 'political union' to run in parallel with the one on economic and monetary union.

When Mrs Thatcher asked them what they meant by political union, she got no clear answer. One reason was that, while both were agreed on the idea of a common foreign policy, which was one of the two specific things to which the term was applied, they

13. Kohl and Mitterrand hold hands among cemeteries where a million French and German soldiers are buried

disagreed about reform of the institutions, which was the other. For while the French wanted to strengthen the intergovernmental elements, in particular the European Council, the Germans wanted to move towards a federal system by strengthening the Parliament. So they could hardly speak with one voice about it. Thatcher wanted neither and, though she accepted the existing EPC, did not want the Community institutions to have a hand in it. While Germany envisaged that foreign policy would move towards becoming a Community competence, France too opposed the idea; and the outcome was the intergovernmental 'second pillar' for a Common Foreign and Security Policy (CFSP).

The CFSP was given a grander name than the EPC and more elaborate institutions. Following Europe's poor showing in the Gulf War, defence was mentioned in the treaty, but in ambiguous terms to accommodate both the French desire for an autonomous European defence capacity and British opposition to any such thing, for fear it could weaken Nato. So nothing much resulted from the use of the word defence. Nor indeed did the CFSP then produce notably better results than the EPC had done before. So there was a second try, in the Amsterdam Treaty, to devise a satisfactory second pillar.

Amsterdam clarified a number of aspects, including a set of general objectives for CFSP, the possibility of using QMV in some cases, as well as enhanced cooperation. Of more consequence was an attempt to provide for a simpler system of external representation, with the creation of a High Representative, a role to be filled by the Secretary General of the Council Secretariat, i.e. an intergovernmental post. Coupled to increased planning capabilities within the Secretariat, this allowed the High Representative, former Nato Secretary-General Javier Solana, to build a much stronger profile in international organizations.

However, Amsterdam and the minor tinkerings of Nice were still insufficient to address the continuing structural problems that

CFSP has faced, and so the Laeken process explicitly focused on the need to engage in a more fundamental reorganization of external representation. This eventually led to the Lisbon Treaty, which ended the Maastricht pillar system and tried to create a single external figure. This new post, the High Representative for the Union for Foreign Affairs and Security Policy, was to join together Commission and Council: the individual would be a vice-president of the former and a chair of the latter's Foreign Affairs formation, as well as attending European Councils. In brief, the High Representative had the potential to become a key international political player, especially with the resources of a new European External Action Service—essentially a European diplomatic corps—behind them. Using the legal framework of the Council's common positions and joint actions, there was great scope to articulate a distinctively European position in the world.

While the reorganization has helped reduce some of the previous complexity and duplication of the system, it would also be fair to say that the choice for the first High Representative of Catherine Ashton also indicated the continuing limits that national leaders have sought to impose. Rather than choosing a high-profile, highly active individual, the decision to have Baroness Ashton signalled a more managerial role for the post. Thus much of her work to date has been taken up with the creation and mobilization of the new Lisbon structures, rather than with conspicuous action. Indeed, the dual institutional roles have meant as much a division of focus as a uniting of policy.

The progressive consolidation of external representation is likely to continue, especially once the new institutions are able to bed in and develop their corporate identities. The growing role for the European Parliament in influencing budget allocations will also surely play a role in this. But it will be in the field of security that the most notable consequences are likely to be felt.

Chart 9 How the EU is represented for Common Foreign and Security Policy

Security

Awareness that the Union should provide more effective military backing for its common policy in former Yugoslavia spurred governments to strengthen its capacity in the field of defence. While recognizing that they depend on Nato and the US for defence against any major threat to their security, they used somewhat stronger language on the Union's own capacity in the Amsterdam Treaty than at Maastricht, envisaging 'the progressive framing of a common defence policy, which might lead to a common defence', the immediate purpose of which was to include humanitarian tasks, peacekeeping, and 'crisis management, including peacemaking'.

This agreement over Nato's role was hard won, in the face of those countries that wished to keep the US out of the picture, the most notable exponent of which was France. It took the difficult experiences of the conflicts in the Balkans, especially in Kosovo, to demonstrate that Europeans, though their defence expenditure amounted to two-thirds that of the Americans, were capable of delivering only one-tenth of the firepower; and their influence over the conduct of the action was correspondingly limited. This brought together the British and French, who had made the principal European contribution, to launch their defence initiative. Experience in the Gulf and the Balkan wars had shown the French that they had to come closer to Nato if they were to make an effective military contribution, while the British for their part had come to see the merit of working with the French; and, having declined to become a founder member of the Eurozone, the government saw defence as a field in which a central role for Britain in the Union could be secured.

The result was the joint proposal for an EU rapid reaction force 'up to' 50,000–60,000 strong, which was adopted by the European Council in Helsinki in December 1999; and it was agreed to integrate WEU into the Union. The EU began to develop a European Security and Defence Policy (ESDP, now referred to as the Common Security and Defence Policy (CSDP)) as the security arm of the CFSP. It established an EU defence planning and staff structure, with Council meetings in which defence ministers participate along with the foreign ministers, a Military Committee representing member states' 'defence chiefs', and military staff within the Council Secretariat; and it converted the Political Committee, responsible to the Council, into a Political and Security Committee. Preparations proceeded for establishing the rapid reaction force, to undertake peacekeeping and crisis management autonomously 'where Nato as a whole is not engaged', though Nato, which in practice meant American, facilities such as air transport and satellite-based intelligence would usually be required; and this means American consent to any substantial operations. Thus the British government's fears about weakening Nato have been allayed; and all member states, including Austria, Finland, Ireland, and Sweden, with their traditions of neutrality, were reassured by the provisions that any member state can opt out of, or into, any action. The Lisbon Treaty reaffirmed these goals, putting CSDP under the control of the High Representative.

This illustrates the difficulties confronting the Union's defence capacity. A critical mass of member states must agree to an action before it can be undertaken; for substantial operations that require Nato facilities and hence American consent, the Americans may not agree to what Europeans want to do, which would give rise to tensions within Nato; and where a European critical mass and American agreement are both available, the intergovernmental arrangements may be too weak to devise and manage a successful operation. While Nato's system is also intergovernmental, American hegemonial leadership has caused it to work. There is no hegemon among the member states; and while this makes it more feasible to develop the Union as a working democracy, it will at the same time make an intergovernmental system in the field of defence hard to operate.

The Union's development in a field so sensitive for sovereignty can hardly be expected to run smoothly. But it encountered rougher waters following al-Qaeda's terrorist attack on the United States in September 2001, when relationships between states were disrupted both in Nato and within the Union itself. The Americans adopted a more unilateralist approach, with the 'war on terror', accompanied by the intervention in Iraq in March 2003; and the Union's member states were sharply divided, with the British, Italian, Polish, and Spanish governments leading the support for the American intervention, while the French and Germans, shortly to be joined by the Italians and Spaniards after changes of government, led those against it. This might have been expected to obstruct the continued development of the Union's capacity in the field of military security as well as relationships within Nato; and it did delay progress of the ESDP for a while. But the Union continued to develop its capacity in the field of security and by 2004 was able to replace Nato's peacekeeping force in Bosnia, to establish the European Defence Agency (EDA) in order to improve the efficiency of arms production, and to create a set of battle groups, each 1,500 strong, intended to be deployable within five days of a Council decision to launch an operation.

As the Union develops its capacity in the field of security, it will become something more than a great civilian power. But its strength in the economic, environmental, and other aspects of external policy, somewhat condescendingly called 'soft power', is already very important, and has great further potential as a force for the development of a safer and more prosperous world.

Chapter 9
The EU and the rest of Europe

A most impressive aspect of the European Union project has been its ability to develop and expand from a small group of relatively similar states in Western Europe into a European Union of much greater width and depth. The process of deepening and widening since the 1950s, with its synergies and contradictions, has been recounted in Chapter 2. Within this long process of enlargement, it is the expansion into Central and Eastern Europe that has, apart from de Gaulle's reaction to the British application, been the most contentious. While member states generally agreed that Eastern enlargement was to be welcomed, to extend the area of prosperity and security, there have also been greatly varying degrees of enthusiasm, to the point where discussion of 'enlargement fatigue' became not uncommon in the old member states. Certainly, there have been problems on the way, but enlargement can be seen as an essential part of the EU and its continued development, not least in its dealings with those who remain outside; and the treaty still affirms that membership is open to any European state that respects 'the principles of liberty, democracy, respect for human rights and fundamental freedoms, and the rule of law'.

Enlargement to almost all of Western Europe

There is a routine for the process of enlargement. When an application is received, the Council asks the Commission for its

'Opinion', on the basis of which the Council may, unanimously, approve a mandate for negotiations. The Commission negotiates, supervised by the Council; and an eventual treaty of accession has to be adopted by unanimity in the Council and with the assent of the Parliament, followed by ratification in all the member states.

Membership can be preceded by a form of association. The original example was the Treaty of Association between Greece and the Community in 1962, which provided for the removal of trade barriers over a transitional period, various forms of cooperation, and a Council of Association. It also envisaged eventual membership; and after various vicissitudes, Greece did indeed become a member in 1981.

Portugal and Spain were not eligible for association in the 1960s. Their regimes were incompatible with the Community, for which only democratic countries were suitable partners; and Portugal had already in 1960 become a founder member of the European Free Trade Association (Efta), which Britain had promoted in reaction to the establishment of the EEC and which, being confined to a purely trading relationship, was not so concerned about the political complexion of its members. So when democracy replaced dictatorship in the 1970s, both Iberian countries negotiated entry to the Community without any prior form of association. This was one reason why the negotiations were protracted, with entry achieved only in 1986. Protectionist resistance, from French farmers in particular, was, however, more significant.

The path to membership was different for the more northerly members of Efta. The British, Danes, Norwegians, Swedes, and Swiss had eschewed the political implications of Community membership; and the Austrians were precluded by their peace treaty. Britain, Denmark, and Ireland joined in 1973 without having been associated in any way. Bilateral free trade agreements were at the same time concluded between the Community and each of the other Efta states, which by then included Iceland; and they were later signed with Finland, which joined in 1986, and Liechtenstein, in 1991.

As soon as the Soviet constraint was removed in 1989, Austria applied for EC membership. Finland, Norway, Sweden, and Switzerland were not far behind. Delors, hoping to delay such enlargement lest it dilute the Community, devised a proposal for a European Economic Area (EEA) to include the Efta countries with the EC in an extended single market. But the governments of those five did not want to be excluded from decision-taking in the Community, so they all applied for membership, which Austria, Finland, and Sweden achieved in 1995, after a short negotiation facilitated by their existing free trade relationship. Norwegians rejected accession in their referendum and Swiss voters refused to accept even the EEA. So Switzerland continues with its bilateral free trade agreement and only a vestigial EEA remains, associating Norway, Iceland, and Liechtenstein with the Union.

Enlargement to the East

Throughout the Cold War, relations were cool between the EC and the Soviet Union. The Soviet Union refused to accord the Community legal recognition, seeing it as strengthening the 'capitalist camp'; and the Community refused to negotiate with Comecon, the economic organization dominated by the Soviet Union. Following 1989, and the dissolution of the Soviet bloc, the Central and East European countries turned towards the Community, which they saw as a bastion of prosperity, democracy, and protection from a chaotic (and collapsing) Soviet Union. They naturally envisaged membership.

The simplest case was the German Democratic Republic, as the Soviet-controlled part of Germany had called itself. The GDR became part of the Federal Republic of Germany in 1990; and the Community made the necessary technical adjustments at speed so

14. The Berlin Wall comes down

that the enlarged Germany could assume the German membership without delay.

For the other countries of Central and Eastern Europe, extensive aid and development packages were put together under the Commission's leadership. Projects such as PHARE sought to provide assistance with economic and political restructuring for the emergent democracies, spending roughly €600 million per year between 1990 and 2003, when it was wound up. However, such assistance, while welcome, was seen by many in the region as a diversion from membership. Indeed, such a view was an accurate reflection of the ambivalence felt by many of the Union's members about enlargement. While publicly proclaiming the historic mission of the Union to reunite Europe peacefully, many politicians were concerned about the admission of a large number of relatively poor, relatively small, and relatively unstable new members, whose populations might move en masse to the West to find employment.

It was only in 1993, at the Copenhagen European Council, that the Union agreed the principle of offering full membership to those who wanted it. However, the Union also agreed for the first time to expand on the provisions of the treaty and laid out what became known as the Copenhagen criteria: stable democracy, human rights and protection of minorities, the rule of law, a competitive market economy, and 'ability to take on the obligations of membership including adherence to the aims of political, economic and monetary union'. While political union meant different things in different member states, the significance of 'the obligations of membership' was clear enough, including the huge task of applying not far short of 100,000 pages of legislation, mostly concerning the single market. To allay fears that widening would result in weakening, there was also the condition that the Union should have 'the capacity to absorb new members while maintaining the momentum of integration'.

Despite this laying out of the threshold for membership, and the development of extensive programmes of assistance to the states of Central and Eastern Europe in order to help meet them, it was only after the conclusion of the Amsterdam Treaty in 1997 that things really started to move. In 1998, the Union judged that a first wave of five had made the necessary progress, so negotiations began in 1998 with the Czech Republic, Estonia, Hungary, Poland, and Slovenia, as well as Cyprus, which had also applied to join; and, in 2000, also with a second wave comprising Bulgaria, Latvia, Lithuania, Romania, and Slovakia, as well as Malta. While the Union had indicated that each individual accession negotiation would proceed at its own speed, it was agreed at the 2003 Copenhagen European Council that all save Bulgaria and Romania would be able to join in May 2004. These two were able to become members in 2007.

The process of enlargement to the East was very protracted, for a number of reasons. On the part of the new member states, the adjustments required were very substantial, especially within the context of emerging from Communist, planned economy systems.

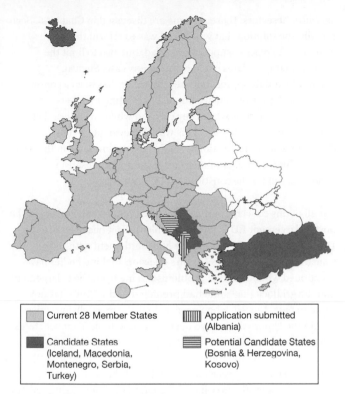

Current 28 Member States

Candidate States
(Iceland, Macedonia,
Montenegro, Serbia,
Turkey)

Application submitted
(Albania)

Potential Candidate States
(Bosnia & Herzegovina,
Kosovo)

Map 2. Applicants for accession

Many states simply lacked the institutions, resources, or experience
necessary to implement fundamental changes in the operation of
many areas of public policy and decision-making. On the part of
the existing member states, we have already mentioned the fears
about the increased heterogeneity of the Union and implications of
free movement and of the state of EU policies. This last point was
to take up much of the Union's time in the late 1990s, as it
struggled to reform CAP and cohesion policies to cope with the
imminent arrival of a large number of poor states with significant

agricultural sectors: those reforms are discussed in Chapter 5. Seen broadly, the solution that was found was to reform the policies by changing the types of support provided, but also to limit the amount that new states could claim in any case. Such an apparently unfair approach to new members has been a consistent feature of all previous enlargements, as existing members seek to protect their interests while they can and while an applicant state has little leverage to fight it. This was also evident with the discussions about institutional reform that culminated in the Nice Treaty, which a number of member states found unsatisfactory enough to call for the constitutional Convention.

For all of this concern, perhaps the most remarkable feature of the post-enlargement EU is how unproblematic it has been to date. Despite the failure to replace the Nice settlement with the Constitutional Treaty, the Union's decision-making bodies have functioned without undue problems arising from the enlargement and the gridlock that some had predicted in the 1990s has not come to pass. Indeed, when we consider the most obvious crises within the Union, these have been more about old member states than new ones: the French and Dutch 'no' votes on the Constitutional Treaty; the Anglo-French split over the Iraq War and its aftermath; Greece's membership of the euro. Partly this has been because the new members have kept a low profile as they learn the ropes of how to work within the Union, with Poland something of an exception; but it is also partly driven by the depth of structural adjustment that these states have made to become members: several of them have been more compliant with the requirements of membership than those they have joined.

South-Eastern Europe

Before it disintegrated, the former Yugoslavia had been closer to the Community than any other Central or East European state. Then came the disintegration and the wars. The United States initially wanted the Europeans to deal with the problems. Jacques

Poos, Luxembourg's Foreign Minister and President-in-Office of the Council in the first half of 1991, famously said, 'This is the hour of Europe.' Slovenia secured independence without much fighting, but bitter wars ensued in Croatia, Bosnia, and later in Kosovo, and in all three cases the Union failed completely to match Poos's claim. Instead, it was the US and Nato that were the main actors in securing a durable peace settlement in the region, the EU being relegated to providing humanitarian relief.

The key consequence of this for the Union was to stimulate a complete review of the Common Foreign and Security Policy, most notably with the creation of hard military capabilities in order to secure the so-called Petersberg tasks of humanitarian relief, peacekeeping, and crisis management. It also helped to make the Union consider how its various external policies linked up together, most obviously seen in the creation of the High Representative to give a single face to the EU's work. As far as the Balkans were concerned, the result of the EU's initial failure was a return to the drawing board and the production of a Stability Pact for South-East Europe. This overarching set of policies, designed to strengthen democracy, human rights, and economic reform, was later followed by Stability and Association Agreements between the Union and each of the West Balkan states. This is backed by the Union's Instrument for Pre-Accession Assistance, which provides some €500 million per year for the West Balkans. With the slow stabilization of the region, the Union has been able to offer membership to Croatia; full candidate status to Macedonia, Montenegro, and Serbia; and a provisional status to the others with Stability and Association Agreements, thus providing a strong incentive for local politicians to follow the example of the other Central and East Europeans.

Russia and the CIS

The three Baltic republics of the former Soviet Union, Estonia, Latvia, and Lithuania, declined to join Russia in the successor

Commonwealth of Independent States (CIS) and became EU members in 2004. Among the states that stayed with the CIS, six can claim to be European: Armenia, Belarus, Georgia, Moldova, Ukraine, and Russia itself. They could therefore, if they come to fulfil the conditions of stable democracy and competitive market economy, apply for membership of the Union.

As the EU has enlarged itself to the borders of Russia and Ukraine, the question of enlargement to CIS states has been raised. The size of Russia, however, combined with the much greater economic and political disparities with the EU than those found in Central and Eastern Europe, stand in the way. The policy has therefore been to develop closer bilateral and multilateral relations rather than to envisage membership. The other states too face great difficulties. But although Ukraine faces major problems in becoming a stable democracy, the desire for membership is not, in the long term, unrealistic.

The EU has, however, long been eager to help with the transition to democracy and free-market economics throughout the CIS. From 1991 until 2007, the Union operated a very extensive programme of assistance known as Technical Assistance to the Commonwealth of Independent States (TACIS). With a budget of around €500 million a year, TACIS concentrated on such things as enterprise restructuring and development, administrative reform, social services, education, and, as the biggest item, nuclear safety, which accounts for a large part of the regional programmes. As will be seen in Chapter 10, TACIS has been superseded by the European Neighbourhood Policy.

The Union's relationship with Russia remains an ambiguous one. While the military rivalry of the Cold War has largely gone, the uncertain nature of Russian democracy under Vladimir Putin in the new century has created new points of tension. As Russia's

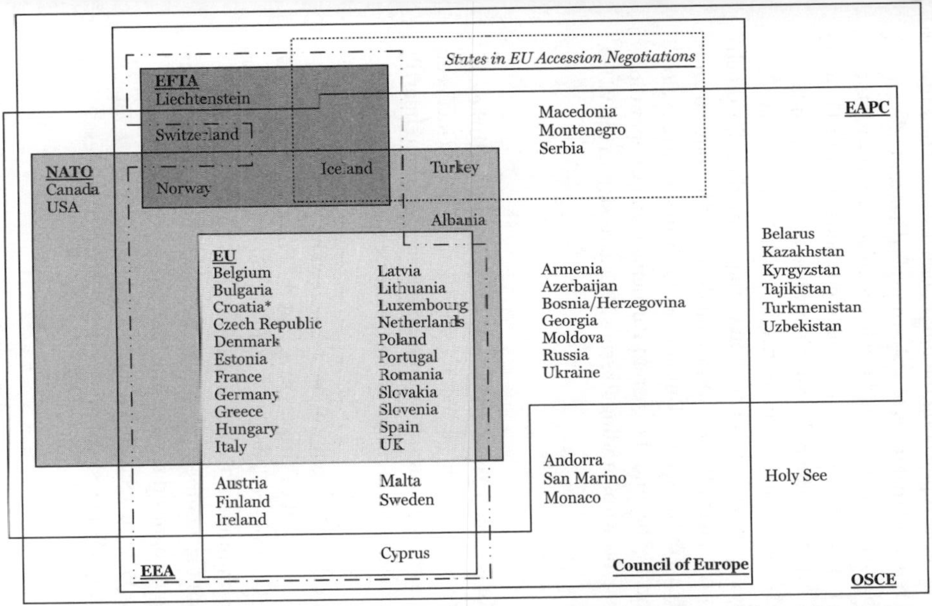

States in EU Accession Negotiations

EAPC

EFTA
Liechtenstein
Switzerland
Norway

Iceland

Turkey

Albania

NATO
Canada
USA

EU
Belgium
Bulgaria
Croatia*
Czech Republic
Denmark
Estonia
France
Germany
Greece
Hungary
Italy

Latvia
Lithuania
Luxembourg
Netherlands
Poland
Portugal
Romania
Slovakia
Slovenia
Spain
UK

Macedonia
Montenegro
Serbia

Armenia
Azerbaijan
Bosnia/Herzegovina
Georgia
Moldova
Russia
Ukraine

Belarus
Kazakhstan
Kyrgyzstan
Tajikistan
Turkmenistan
Uzbekistan

EEA

Austria
Finland
Ireland

Malta
Sweden

Cyprus

Andorra
San Marino
Monaco

Holy See

Council of Europe

OSCE

EAPC = Euro-Atlantic Partnership Council; EEA = European Economic Area; EFTA = European Free Trade Area; EU = European Union; NATO = North Atlantic Treaty Organization; OSCE = Organization for Security and Cooperation in Europe. * = Croatia became a member of the EU in July 2013.

Map 3. The architecture of Europe, 2013

121

military might has faded and the shift to free-market economics has not yet been as successful as hoped, so the Russian government has started to use its massive natural energy exports to Europe as a new way of being a player on the international scene. The Putin era has seen repeated instances of state-controlled gas and oil companies using their size and privileged relationship with the Kremlin to gain increasingly dominant positions within EU energy markets, helped by the EU's own energy liberalization agenda. While this dominance is conditioned by the fact that Russian companies are now dependent upon European markets for much of their profits, until there is more confidence in the political and legal systems in Russia, the Union is not likely to seek to develop its relationship beyond the current Partnership and Cooperation Agreement, notwithstanding Russia's 2012 accession to the WTO.

Turkey

We cannot complete this chapter without reference to Turkey. If Russia is a problematic partner for the EU, then Turkey has been more like a thorn in its side, because it has so openly and heartily wished to become a member of the Union for such a long time.

Turkey concluded a Treaty of Association with the EEC in 1964, which was like that of Greece, save that the Community's doubts about Turkey were reflected in a transition period of 22 years and no clear commitment to membership. Turkey lodged its application for membership in 1987, but it was not until 1999 that the Union recognized it as a candidate, and negotiations began only in 2005, with accession not expected for many years yet. Even by the EU's low standards, such a protracted process requires some explanation.

Union politicians have voiced a number of reasons for doubting whether Turkey should become a member. First, there has been reference to the Copenhagen criteria and the country's unsuitability on the grounds of human rights abuses, the role of the military in politics, weaknesses in the economy, and the extent to which reforms can meaningfully be made. Second, there are concerns regarding the size of Turkey (it would before long be the EU's largest member state, owing to its high birth rate) and the resultant potential for large-scale migration to other member states and for voting weight in the Council. Third, there has been much talk of 'enlargement fatigue' and the need for a more substantial pause before such a major expansion. Fourth, and perhaps underlining all of these other dimensions, is the notion of Turkey's 'otherness'. As a majority Muslim population, as a state with a tenuous claim to be geographically 'European', and as a state with a very different historical path from that of current members, it challenges many conceptions of what the EU is and should be.

For the Turks' part, their persistence in the face of such opposition reflects the strength of the Western Kemalist project in the country and of its self-conception as a bridge between East and West. Certainly, successive Turkish governments have made very extensive modifications to legal and political structures in order to secure the accession negotiations that they so desired, something that is all the more surprising for the lack of certainty that such negotiations would occur. However, Turkish patience, especially in the general public, is not infinite, and in recent years there has been a cooling in the desire to join the Union. Again, this is a standard feature of enlargements: as membership draws closer, people begin to see the costs as well as the benefits.

Nonetheless, Turkey's membership remains unresolved. In many member states, Turkish membership is deeply problematic, both for publics and for elites. However, the question has to be asked of whether or not excluding Turkey is desirable. The EU already has over 15 million Muslims, so religion is not the barrier that some imagine. Likewise, admitting Turkey could help consolidate the EU's status as a global power, both through the admission of a state that bridges into the Middle East and through its extensive military capability. Whatever decision is finally made, it will have serious implications for the Union and its future development.

Chapter 10
The EU in the world

Having shown how 'federal institutions can unite highly developed states', the Community might serve as an example of how 'to create a more prosperous and peaceful world'. Such was the hope that Jean Monnet expressed in 1954 to the students of Columbia University in New York. The EU has been concerned, like others, to look after its own interests, even if it is often hard to reach agreement on what these are. But Europeans have become more aware than most others that these do include the creation of a prosperous and peaceful world. How do its actions, as distinct from its example as a region of peace and welfare, contribute to that end?

The Community as a great trading power

The United States sponsored the uniting of Europe, from Marshall Aid to the birth and early development of the Community. Monnet reciprocated with the idea of an increasingly equal EC–US partnership. Soon after the EEC was founded with its common external tariff, the US responded by initiating the Kennedy Round of trade liberalization in the Gatt; and this led in 1967, after five years of laborious negotiations, to the agreement to cut tariffs by one-third.

That would have been out of the question had the Community not become, with its common tariff as an instrument of external policy, a trading partner on level terms with the US. As an observer in Washington put it, the EC was 'now the most important member of Gatt', and the key to further efforts to liberalize trade. So it indeed became in later rounds of Gatt negotiations, as the creative American impulse of the post-war period declined. The Community played the leading part in the Uruguay Round, concluded in 1994. With tariffs on most manufactures already low, the focus moved to non-tariff barriers where the single market programme gave the Community a unique experience in techniques of liberalization. Its experience was also relevant to the replacement of the Gatt by the World Trade Organization, with its wider scope and greater powers for resolving disputes: a step, perhaps, towards validating the suggestion that the EC's 'example of effective international law-making' might at some stage be 'replicated at global level'.

Of course the Community's trade relations have engendered the normal clash of interests, or at least of what participants suppose to be their interests, with agriculture the prime bone of contention. The protectionist common agricultural policy damaged trading partners such as Australia, Canada, New Zealand, and the US. Following UK accession, this was particularly harmful to the first three, a blow that could have been avoided had Britain not failed to join when the Rome Treaty was negotiated. It was not until the 1990s that the Community began to carry out serious reform, when it cut the level of protection for some major items by about half; and it was agreed in the Uruguay Round that the trade-disrupting export subsidies would be eliminated in the following round: a tough challenge for both the Community and the United States.

While moving closer together on agriculture, the Community and the US diverged over environmental, cultural, and consumer protection issues, with the Europeans favouring standards which led to restriction of their imports from the US and which the Americans regarded as protectionist. Genetically modified organisms, hormone-treated beef, noisy aero-engines, data privacy, and films and television programmes were cases in point.

The friction induced by the Union's network of preferential arrangements has, on the contrary, been eased as tariffs were reduced in successive Gatt rounds. That network had become so extensive, covering almost the whole of Europe and the less-developed countries, that only a few remained outside it, including Australia, Canada, Japan, New Zealand, South Africa, and the US. The Americans were irked by the EC's preferences for particular countries. But the other side of this coin was the relationships that the EC established with large parts of the world's South, which were, however, put to a hard test in the Doha Round of trade negotiations that opened in 2001, with the EU wanting a comprehensive agenda and the US preferring to concentrate on fields such as agriculture and the environment.

The Union's desire to include matters such as investment, competition policy, public procurement, and trade facilitation, known as the 'Singapore issues', was motivated partly by the view that the world should start moving, as the EU itself had done, beyond the focus on tariffs and import quotas in order to deal with other areas of policy that have a growing impact on trade. But developing countries were not ready for this; and their negotiating power was enhanced by the creation of the G20, led by Brazil, China, India, and South Africa, with others representing regional and trading interests. Agriculture also emerged, as usual, as an obstacle, with the European and American farm lobbies resisting liberalization; and for some less-developed countries there was an additional problem arising from the Union's 'everything but arms' decision to abolish restrictions on imports from the 40 poorest countries, to the detriment of their competitors in other less-developed countries.

By May 2004 the Trade Commissioner, Pascal Lamy, was able to offer to reduce the Union's insistence on the Singapore issues and to negotiate the removal of all export subsidies, thus enabling the negotiations to move forward in that year. At the same time a surge in imports of clothing from China gave a foretaste of the scale of the challenges to be expected to follow from the size of the Chinese economy and the speed of its growth, with similar impact from India likely to follow; and Chinese accession to the WTO in 2001 was to make it harder for the Union to react with anti-dumping measures.

Since then Doha has floundered on the rocks of intransigent behaviour on all sides and is currently deadlocked on a number of basic issues. Whatever the ultimate outcome, there will be consideration of the viability of further trade rounds that have to be approved unanimously by 150 states, and of whether a different route towards international trade liberalization will be required; and the Union will have to consider whether, and if so how, its own experience of the last half-century can be applied in the wider world.

The EU, its neighbourhood, and the developing world

Whereas relations with the US are important for all member states, individual states have special relationships with particular countries in most of the rest of the world; and many of these became shared by the Union as a whole.

This, like much else, stems from the Treaty of Rome. France wanted advantages for its colonies, and made this a condition for ratification of the treaty. So the Community as a whole granted free entry to imports from them and provided aid through the European Development Fund (EDF). The same applied to territories relating to Belgium, Italy, and the Netherlands; and the resulting association was the original basis for the present Cotonou Convention. French pressure also led to preferential agreements for Morocco and Tunisia; and these were the forerunners of the present far-reaching system of agreements with neighbouring states.

After they became independent, the association with former colonies was transmuted through a Convention that provided for joint institutions: a Council of Ministers, Committee of Ambassadors, and Assembly of Parliamentarians. Following British accession, the Commonwealth countries of Africa, the Caribbean, and the Pacific joined in negotiating the Lomé Convention. This broadened the participation to include most of Africa and the Caribbean islands, as well as a number of islands in the Pacific, known collectively as the ACP countries. It removed some vestiges of the colonial system and has expanded the aid towards a level of €3 billion a year since the 1990s, together with money to cushion the associates against falls in their income from commodity exports.

The Lomé Convention was renewed for the fifth time at Cotonou in the year 2000, in difficult circumstances. For the associates were disturbed by the erosion of the margins of preference as tariffs had been reduced in successive Gatt rounds; and the Union was concerned that, despite the massive quantities of aid, almost all of Africa remained in bad shape, owing at least partly to poor governance. Enough was at stake, however, to win the agreement to the fifth Convention, both of the EU's 79 African, Caribbean, and Pacific (ACP) partners, with the renewal of the aid programme, and of its member states, with the Convention's recognition that adequate performance in governance would be a criterion for the allocation of aid, and that the associates were to prepare their economies to join the Union in a free trade area in 20 years' time. Through the 1990s, moreover, the EU laid growing emphasis in its external relations on human rights, and the Cotonou Convention requires the participants to respect them.

By the end of the 1970s the Community also had a network of agreements according preferences and assistance to states around

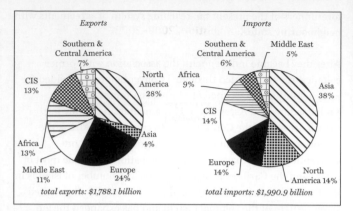

Chart 10 Direction of EU trade in goods by region, 2010

the Mediterranean, with content not unlike that of the Lomé Convention but without the multilateral institutions. The network included all the North African states—save Libya which declined to participate—together with Israel, Lebanon, and, at one remove from the Mediterranean, Jordan and Syria.

By the 1990s, a combination of economic difficulties, political instability, and rapid population growth in most of these countries, with consequent pressure to migrate to Europe, caused growing anxiety in the Union, particularly among its southern states. The outcome was a conference of ministers from the Union and its Mediterranean partners, held in Barcelona in 1995, which launched a 'Euro-Mediterranean process' aimed at building a wide range of multilateral links across the basin. However, the headline goal of the process—a free trade area by 2005—was soon to founder on the political differences of the partners and the constant distraction of the Eastern enlargement.

With the coming of that enlargement, the Union engaged in a wholesale review of its links with its neighbours, with a particular eye on trying to keep the Union an open and accessible grouping.

Box 5 Cotonou Convention, 2000–2020

The EU and ACP states agreed in 2000 to renew the Lomé
Convention for the fifth time, for a 20-year period. The resultant
Cotonou Convention is revised every five years and the aid
protocols are also limited to five-year periods. The ACP-EU Council
of Ministers meets yearly to review progress.

- *Trade* is at the heart of the agreement. Negotiations between
  the EU and each ACP state for 'economic partnership
  agreements' are to result eventually in new trading
  arrangements (Economic Partnership Agreements) intended
  to lead to an EU-ACP free trade area by 2020. Meanwhile the
  free or preferential entry to the EU is to be retained.
- *Aid* was set at €13.5 billion for 2000–7, on top of €9.5 billion
  already allocated but not yet spent. Good performance in use
  of aid is to be rewarded.
- *Poverty reduction* is to be a favoured focus for development
  strategies.
- *Non-state actors* are to be encouraged to participate in the
  development process.
- *Political dialogue* indicates a harder-nosed EU approach, with
  good governance, respect for human rights, democratic
  principles, and the rule of law as criteria for aid policy, and
  with action against corruption.

Cotonou is coloured by the EU's disappointment with the results
of the preceding Lomé Conventions, attributed to poor
governance in many countries. Given this starting point, the
development of an EU-ACP free trade area is a very ambitious idea
and one that has already slipped behind schedule.

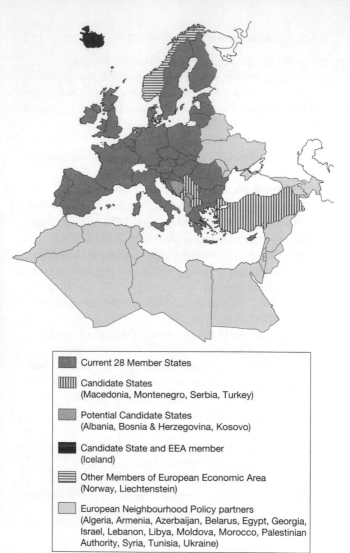

The European Union

	Current 28 Member States
	Candidate States (Macedonia, Montenegro, Serbia, Turkey)
	Potential Candidate States (Albania, Bosnia & Herzegovina, Kosovo)
	Candidate State and EEA member (Iceland)
	Other Members of European Economic Area (Norway, Liechtenstein)
	European Neighbourhood Policy partners (Algeria, Armenia, Azerbaijan, Belarus, Egypt, Georgia, Israel, Lebanon, Libya, Moldova, Morocco, Palestinian Authority, Syria, Tunisia, Ukraine)

Map 4. The EU's neighbourhood

Thus it was in 2003 that the Commission proposed replacing the Euro-Mediterranean process, PHARE, and TACIS with a European Neighbourhood Policy. In 2007, these former programmes were formally incorporated into the ENP, supported by a new financial instrument that will provide some €1.7 billion a year for cross-border cooperation, the development of civil society, and technical assistance.

While the ENP represents a significant commitment on the part of the EU to these countries, it remains to be seen whether it will have any significant impact on the development of a more stable, democratic, or prosperous environment around the EU's borders, especially in light of the Arab spring of 2011 and the continued weakness of governance in several East European states.

Asia, Latin America, and generalized preferences

Britain, on joining the Community, managed to secure satisfactory terms for Commonwealth countries from Africa, the Caribbean, and the Pacific. But no special arrangement was agreed for the Asian members of the Commonwealth—India, Pakistan (which then included Bangladesh), Sri Lanka, Malaysia, Hong Kong, and Singapore—most of whose exports had entered Britain tariff-free under Commonwealth preference. The damage was limited, however, because in 1971 the Community was among the first to adopt a Generalized System of Preferences (GSP), according preferential entry to imports from almost all Third World countries that did not already benefit from the Lomé Convention or the Mediterranean agreements; and this reduced the discrimination against most Asian and Latin American countries. The system was less favourable than it may sound because for 'sensitive' (that is, the more competitive) products there were quotas limiting the preferences to quantities fixed in advance for each product and each member state. But the generalized preferences nevertheless helped to strengthen links with less-developed countries.

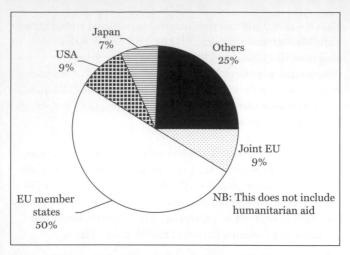

Chart 11 Shares of official development aid from EU, US, Japan, and others, 2011

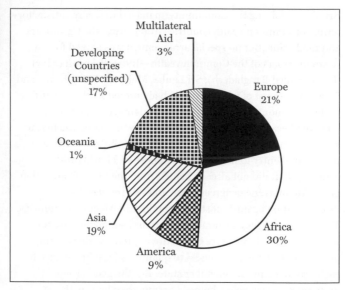

Chart 12 Development aid from EU and member states by destination, 2010

Box 6 EU agreements and links in the Third World, other than Cotonou and ENP

The EU has Trade and Cooperation Agreements with:

Argentina	Mexico	South Korea
Brazil	Pakistan	Sri Lanka
Chile	Paraguay	Uruguay
Colombia	South Africa	Vietnam
India		

The EU has links with other regional groupings, including:

Andean Community (South America)	Gulf Cooperation Council
Mercosur (South America)	SAARC (South Asian Association for Regional Cooperation)
San José group (Central America)	ASEAN (Association of South-East Asian Nations)

The EU's Generalized System of Preferences applies to almost all developing countries.

While the margins of preference that the GSP affords less-developed countries have declined along with the reduction of the general level of tariffs, their links with the EU through its aid programmes have become increasingly important. These amount to some €10 billion a year, including both humanitarian aid and the development aid for ACP countries and the ENP. The Union has also concluded bilateral trade and cooperation agreements to strengthen its links with major developing countries, including

India, Mexico, and Brazil; it has agreements with regional groups such as ASEAN (the Association of South-East Asian Nations); and since Portugal and Spain joined the Community in 1986, their special links with Latin America have been added to those of other member states in Africa and Asia.

While the economic impact of the agreements, preferences, and aid can hardly be measured and may not have been very great, the Union has gained political credit which may be of help in the future development of its relationships with Asian, African, and Latin American countries.

Money

Whereas its common tariff had made the Union a trading power equivalent to the US, before the euro it had no monetary instrument that could become the equal of the dollar in the international monetary system. The challenge to American hegemony was one of the motives behind the long-standing French support for a single currency. The fluctuations of dollar exchange rates were uncomfortable for other member states too. The dollar's weakness first disrupted the attempt to create a single currency in the early 1970s, then spurred Europeans into taking the first major step of monetary integration with the establishment of the European Monetary System in 1979. In the 1980s the US policy of high interest rates, designed to counter inflation, provoked a debt crisis in many developing countries, restricting their development for up to a decade.

When those who manage a dominant currency have to choose between dealing with a domestic problem and taking account of the impact on other economies that are influenced by their choice, they naturally choose their domestic interests. Europeans experienced this in the 1990s when high German interest rates, designed to control inflation following German unification, exacerbated recession in other countries influenced by the dominant Deutschmark; and this gave added edge to their support for the single currency, with a monetary policy tailored to the needs of the participants as a whole. While that remedy is not available to deal with the dollar's dominance in the world system, the euro has developed into a significant countervailing monetary power, the Eurozone crisis notwithstanding.

Thus the euro is another source of money with a different economic cycle, which can counteract the dollar's influence when it works against other countries' interests. This has been limited by two main factors. First, there is still an unclear arrangement for conducting external monetary policy, the responsibility being divided between the European Central Bank and the Council of finance ministers. Second, the continuing structural problems presented by the Eurozone crisis have also proved a very major distraction. So the Union has not yet made full use of the opportunity that the euro offers to replace American hegemony with a more equal relationship, such as the common commercial policy has long since done with respect to trade.

Security: peacekeeping and climate change

American hegemony in defence will, however, remain unchallenged for as long ahead as can be contemplated. Not only would Europeans have to undertake vast expenditure in any attempt to become independent of American strategic power, but the force thus acquired would also have to be controlled by a solidly established democratic European state with a number of years of reliable decision-taking behind it. So Europeans continue to depend on Nato's American-led strategic shield; and their efforts in the field of defence will be mainly to contribute to peacekeeping and peacemaking, particularly in actions sponsored by the United Nations. For defence of the Union's territory against major threats, Europeans will continue to depend on American protection.

It would be unwise to assume that such protection would never be needed, in what is becoming a multipolar world in strategic as well as economic terms, and where a growing number of states have weapons of mass destruction. Military threats to the Union's interests could, moreover, emerge with which the Americans may be unable or unwilling to deal. So the Union is likely to continue building its defence capacity as well as to keep the alliance in repair, while at the same time using its soft power to further the development of a safer world.

The Union did, as we saw in Chapter 8, resume the development of its military activities without much delay, following the internal divisions during the build-up to the American intervention in Iraq. In 2003, the European Council unanimously approved an EU strategy to strengthen security around the Union and in the international order. In 2004, the Nato force in Bosnia was replaced by the EU force of 7,000 troops, with Nato assets and capabilities; and smaller but significant operations were undertaken in Georgia, Macedonia, and the Democratic Republic of Congo—the latter a precursor of the project for establishing battle groups which was launched in the same year. By 2006, the Union sent a peacekeeping force of some 8,000 troops to Lebanon after the war there between Hizbollah and Israel. Since 2008, the EU has also provided substantial resources to combating piracy in Somalia with its Atalanta mission.

Thus the Union continued creating a significant capacity for military contributions to peacekeeping and peacemaking, a most important complement to which is its capacity to contribute to the civilian elements of peacekeeping, together with its experience in assisting the building of democratic states. One example, which can follow directly from a successful military mission, is the police missions, such as the Union has provided in Bosnia, where in 2003 it took over from a UN Police Task Force, followed by others in Macedonia, Democratic Republic of Congo, and Palestinian Territories. More broadly, it has much experience of assisting with the development of political, judicial, and administrative institutions, and the structures of civil society, particularly among

Central and East European states preparing themselves for accession, as well as in the West Balkans and farther afield; and this has great potential importance for wider application in a world in which failed or failing states can be a serious security risk, while solidly based democracies can contribute much to stable international relations.

The environment is also a vital aspect of security, with climate change among the gravest threats to the welfare, and perhaps the lives, of the world's people; and the Union has made the major contribution to international efforts to deal with it. In 1986, when it had become evident that chlorofluorocarbons (CFCs) could destroy the ozone layer and thus endanger life on Earth, the EC succeeded in breaking a deadlock in negotiations for the Montreal Protocol to the UN Framework Convention on Climate Change (UNFCCC), thus halting the degradation. Then in 1997 the Union played the leading part in the negotiations for the UNFCCC's Kyoto Protocol to stem the emissions of carbon dioxide and other greenhouse gases, which are generating a potentially disastrous degree of global warming. Despite intractable American resistance to targets as well as to the assistance required by developing countries for the necessary technological transformation, the EU ensured that there was agreement on the target of cutting emission by 8 per cent below 1990 emissions by 2012. It also secured sufficient ratifications, in the teeth of energetic American opposition, for the Protocol to enter into force in February 2005; and the final ratification required was that of Russia, which appears to have been encouraged by the Union's use of an instrument of its common commercial policy, as the EU almost simultaneously reciprocated with its formal acceptance of Russia's coveted entry into the WTO.

Having concluded that global emissions need to be cut by 60 per cent by mid-century and adopted that target for its own emissions, the EU has a compelling interest in securing similar commitments from as many states as possible. While progress on this front has stalled since the 2009 Copenhagen summit, the Union remains at the forefront of international efforts.

The Union's role in the world

Too much American hegemony is dangerous for Americans as well as for others. Overwhelming power can lead to rash decisions; and the burden is too great for one country to carry alone. China seems likely to catch up with the US during the first half of this century as a military as well as economic power, with unpredictable consequences; and India may well follow. But the EU has the potential to be, much sooner, at least an equal partner with the US with respect to the economy, the environment, and soft security, though not defence.

Indeed, the EU's long-standing parity with the US in the world trading system has shown what can be done when sufficiently effective institutions dispose of a common instrument. The euro

15. The G8 summit, Camp David, May 2012, with President of the European Council, Herman van Rompuy (sitting to the left of Angela Merkel), and Commission President, José Manuel Barroso (to van Rompuy's left)

offers a basis for a similar performance in the international monetary system, if the institutions for external monetary policy are adequately reformed. For action on global climate change the Union should be able, again with some strengthening of its institutions, to maintain its leading role. Soft security, including the civilian aspects of keeping the peace, is a field in which it is developing a capacity that could become an essential counterpart for American military power; and the military instruments that the EU is creating also open up opportunities to perform a complementary role.

Adjustment to such changes in power relationships is always hard for those who have been on top. But it should not be too hard for Americans to adjust to a more powerful European Union, with a society that shares so much in so many ways; with four decades of reasonable cooperation in the field of trade where both already have equivalent strength; and with no prospect of rivalry in the field of military power. Having adjusted to an equal partnership with the EU in most other fields, it should be easier for the US to adjust to changes in relationships with other emergent powers, particularly as the EU will be well placed, with its network of relations with countries around the world, to advance the process of creating a stable world system that accommodates them.

The Union's own experience of institutions, policies, and attitudes that have helped the member states to live together in peace for half a century, together with its worldwide network of relationships, should indeed enable it to influence others to move in a similar direction. But Monnet's idea that such institutions might serve to create a prosperous and peaceful world could be realized only under quite exacting conditions. The necessary sharing of sovereignty is possible only among pluralist democracies that are willing to accept a common rule of law, and have the capacity to develop common legislative institutions to enact it and a system of government to implement policies within it. These conditions apply to a large extent within the Union, but in many parts of the world they do not. Meanwhile the Union can assist efforts to develop such conditions where they do not yet exist and to undertake Union-type developments where they do; and it can support steps to help the United Nations and other international organizations to become more effective, while recognizing that institutions of a Union type cannot be created at that level until pluralist democracy becomes the norm throughout the world. But Union policies which point towards such an outcome are in the long-term interest of its states and citizens; and even if a very long time-scale has to be envisaged, the European experience has shown that initiating a process which leads in that direction can already begin to transform relations between states.

Chapter 11
Much accomplished ... but what next?

The European Union has come a long way since the process of its construction was launched by the Schuman Declaration in 1950. War has indeed become unthinkable among the member states, which now include most European countries. The preceding chapters have shown how institutions, powers, and policies have been put in place to deal with matters beyond the reach of governments of the individual states. But they have also shown that the Union needs further reform if it is to promote the interests of its people adequately in an increasingly problematic world. Now we can try to sum up what has been done and venture some thoughts about the future.

Do the powers and instruments match the aims?

The Union has been able to achieve its aims where it has the powers and instruments as well as the institutions with which to act. The powers and instruments can be legislative, such as the framework for the single market; fiscal, as with the budget or the common external tariff; or financial, as with the aid programmes, the European Investment Bank, and most importantly the single currency. Cooperation based on the powers and instruments of member states can be useful, but would not achieve much without the hard core of common powers and instruments.

The single market legislation provides a framework for economic strength and prosperity, even if it remains incomplete in some significant sectors and will need further development to cater adequately for the new economy including e-commerce and information technology; and, for member states that have adopted the euro, the single currency completes the single market in the monetary domain.

The budget has transferred resources to sectors deemed to require support, originally to agriculture but increasingly to less-developed regions and member states. While the agricultural budget has generated conflict, the structural funds to assist development of poorer regions have been more generally favoured; and the enlargement to Central and Eastern Europe reinforces the case for larger funds.

Thus the Union has many of the necessary powers in the economic field. The same can be said of the environment, where the most pressing need is to strengthen both internal and external action to limit the damage from climate change.

Social policy as embodied in the welfare state belongs largely, following the principle of subsidiarity, to the member states. That principle justifies Union involvement in some employment-related aspects of social policy, such as the prevention of social dumping by undercutting standards of health and safety at work. There is a grey area, including elements of social security and hours of work, where there is conflict between those who want to establish Union-wide standards and those who consider that differences rooted in differing social cultures should not be disturbed. Disagreements remain; but the latter view has gained ground.

While the economic and environmental aims and powers were promoted by interest groups as well as federalists, as was the free movement of workers across the internal frontiers, it was the federal idea that lay behind free movement for all within the Union, which has been accepted, apart from transitional derogations relating to new member states, by all save Denmark, Ireland, and the UK. But all participate in measures to combat cross-frontier crime.

In the field of its external relations, the Union's powers have been designed to defend and promote common interests, which include stability in the international economic and political system. The most potent instrument is the offer of accession, hence of participation in the Union's institutions and powers as a whole. But this is available only for European states; and other means have to be used to advance the Union's interests in the rest of the world.

The powers over external trade, together with the instrument of the common external tariff, have enabled the Union to serve its interest in liberal international trade as well as to turn what was American hegemony in this field into EU–US partnership. The protectionist common agricultural policy, working in the opposite direction, marred relations with many trading partners. Reforms to correct this distortion have taken far too long, but are being accomplished by stages. A combination of preferential arrangements and aid has strengthened links with most Third World countries.

Along with this influence in the world trading system, the Union has used its environmental powers to play the leading part in international negotiations to protect the ozone layer and limit the damage from climate change.

With the euro the Union has a powerful instrument to wield in the international monetary system. But until it has resolved both its internal governance and the basic political and economic challenges posed by the Eurozone crisis, its potential, which could convert American hegemony into partnership in this field too, is not likely to be realized.

For defence, American military dominance remains a fact which the EU's incremental approach to military integration is not designed to challenge, though it serves increasingly useful purposes. It is in the civil domain that the Union can complement American power, with civilian aspects of peacekeeping and, much more substantially, through its contribution to European and world stability in the economic, environmental, and political fields. The Union is uniquely placed to ease the transition from global American hegemony to a multipolar world, in which Euro-American partnership can play an essential part. The Union needs some new powers to accomplish this, together with further reform of the institutions to enable it to use the powers to good effect.

The institutions: how effective? how democratic?

Eurosceptics tend to regard 'closer integration' as undesirable without distinguishing between transfer of powers to the Union and reform of its institutions. But these are two very different questions. The transfer of powers is justified only where the Union can serve the citizens in ways that individual member states cannot; and the Union already has many of the powers indicated by the subsidiarity principle except in the field of defence. Once powers have been transferred, however, they will not serve the citizens' interests well enough unless they are wielded by effective and democratic Union institutions.

The political institutions require a context of the rule of law, which is ensured by the Court of Justice in matters of Union competence; and this has brought fundamental change in the relations among member states.

The Council, however, is not effective enough where the unanimity rule prevails, as was demonstrated by the inadequacy of single market legislation before qualified majority voting was applied. It has become more effective now that QMV applies to the large majority of legislative acts as well as the whole of the budget; and unanimity and enhanced cooperation remain practical procedures where the Union depends on the use of member states' instruments, as in the field of defence. But in line with the growth in the number of member states, there must be increasing doubts about the Union's capacity to act where unanimity still applies, for example with treaties of association and accession, nominations to some major posts in the institutions, and international agreements on exchange rate arrangements.

The Commission has substantial powers to fulfil its functions as the Union's executive, though its role in ensuring that member states do in fact carry out the administration that is delegated to them by the Union is not strong enough, and too much intervention by the Council and its network of committees in the execution of Union decisions hampers the Commission's effectiveness. The Commission's own administrative culture had also become a serious weakness, but the reforms effected after the European Parliament secured the Commission's resignation in March 1999 brought substantial improvement.

The part the Parliament then played in ensuring the Commission's resignation showed how democratic control can contribute to effectiveness. However, the Parliament's powers are still constrained by the treaties. While the Lisbon Treaty did make co-decision into (literally) the Ordinary Legislative Procedure, reflecting its general application, there still remain assorted Special Legislative Procedures; for so long as this remains the case, the Union will be neglecting an essential means of securing citizens' support. Even with their strengthened rights under the Lisbon Treaty, citizens still lack meaningful connection with the Union; and it would be unwise to ignore the track record of representative democracy as a major element in citizenship. So long as citizens do not see the Parliament as an equal of the Council, they are not likely to regard it as a sufficiently important channel of representation. The Council, representing the states, is an essential part of the Union's legislature too. But despite the progress in holding legislative sessions in public, it remains at the centre of an opaque system of quasi-diplomatic negotiation. Representation in a powerful house of the citizens may well be a condition of their support for the Union over the longer term.

The success of the provision for gender equality at work shows how citizens' rights can also generate support for the Union. The incorporation of the Charter of Fundamental Rights and the looming accession of the Union to the European Convention on Human Rights provide some positives. But most important of all for the citizens will be the Union's general effectiveness in doing things that are necessary for them. It must be seen to be doing such things at a time when it confronts major challenges, both internally and in the world at large.

Flexible versus federal

The word 'flexible' is used approvingly in much British discourse on Europe to denote both the avoidance of excessive regulation in the economy and, politically, an aversion to proposals, apart from completion of the single market, for common instruments and legally binding commitments such as characterized the European Community pillar of the Union.

Flexibility in the economic sense has been successful in the development of the swiftly changing contemporary economy; and this has been increasingly recognized in the EU. But flexibility in the political sense is not appropriate for matters which the individual states are unable to handle effectively. The recent challenges to some of the fundamental principles of the Union, including free movement and non-discrimination on the basis of nationality, have demonstrated the need for collective action, the better to protect the rights of all members.

A vital challenge for the longer term is also to ensure that European enterprises will be among the leaders in technological development; and in some sectors such as aircraft and satellites, this requires large and long-term investments of public money: an increasingly difficult proposition in the current economic climate. A common European effort is needed to support such projects, which are too large for single European governments; and in so far as some member states are not ready to participate, there can be structured enhanced cooperation among those that are.

The Eurozone crisis has demonstrated very vividly the extent to which national economies are deeply interlinked and interdependent. Thus the ability of the Eurozone to find lasting solutions to its problems is of interest not only to its members, but also to all other EU member states, and beyond. One of the more difficult messages that has needed to be communicated in the UK is precisely that it is neither possible nor desirable to stand on the sidelines of events and urge others to do something. This is undoubtedly true in economic matters, although it does present many complications in both political and legal terms. As the Fiscal Compact negotiations showed, even if a state is not a signatory, it still needs to be involved in some form. More generally, the Compact also showed that sometimes some member states will want to move ahead of others.

The debate in the UK about withdrawal from the Union has largely been one built on a lack of knowledge and understanding about both the operation of the EU and the nature of global interconnectedness. Even if the UK did leave, it would still find itself neighbouring a Union that bought British goods and services, but in which the British government no longer had an institutional voice (and vote). Moreover, the UK's current position as a desirable entry point to the EU for third countries' businesses would also be undermined. Seen as such, constructive engagement would offer much more likelihood of an acceptable policy mix than would a metaphorical throwing up of the hands.

A large part of the divergence between the approaches of the British and of most other member states has stemmed from the differing experiences in World War Two, which was more traumatic for most of the continental nations. So while much of the progress in building the Union has had economic motives, it was a profound desire to consolidate peace and security that underlay the major shifts towards the sharing of sovereignty, such as the European Coal and Steel Community, and the Treaties of Rome and Maastricht. The British accepted the merits of economic integration but resisted the sharing of sovereignty, accepting only what was required to participate in the large market or to avoid losing too much political influence.

But governments and large numbers of citizens throughout the Union, including the British, are conscious of the many and various sources of insecurity in the world, and share the desire for progress towards a safer world based on a more effective multilateral system. So they may also be able to accept the implication of such sharing of sovereignty as may be necessary in order to enhance sufficiently the Union's capacity for action towards that end. Its military capabilities for peacekeeping are growing; and while it is not likely to become a great military power, it can become the world's principal peacemaker across an impressive range of soft power. It can enhance its contribution to prosperity and stability in the global economy in the fields of trade, aid, and external monetary policy; it can help, as it has shown in the West Balkans and elsewhere, to build and sustain viable democratic states; and it has led the world in action to prevent ruinous climate change. It could moreover do much, as a very great civilian power, to ease the transition to a world in which the United States will be joined by China, then India, as very great powers in the military sense too; and it can help them and others to develop an increasingly effective United Nations.

There is a wide consensus among member states, not least the UK, about the validity of such aims. But there has not been agreement on how to apply the Union's full weight in achieving them. A major difficulty has been the reluctance of many, again not least the British, to accept the allocation of resources to the Union and to strengthen its institutions in ways that could make it sufficiently effective; and this implies the acceptance of an adequate core of legally binding commitments and common instruments, with institutional reform to make the Union properly effective and democratic. The word 'federal' is a convenient and accurate abbreviation for the words following 'core of' in the preceding sentence, whether or not such commitments, instruments, and reformed institutions lead eventually to a federation. The word is less important than what it represents. Its use, if properly defined, would, however, clarify thinking as well as facilitate communication with those who use it. A rose by any other name would smell as sweet. But it is better to give the rose a name consisting of one word rather than seventeen.

The British, as much as other Europeans, sense their exposure to the mounting sources of insecurity in the world today. So Britain should be able to play a fully constructive part in supporting reforms of the Union's existing powers and institutions that would enable it to realize its great potential influence towards creating a safer and more prosperous world.

References

References, in line with the nature of this series, have been kept to the minimum of quotations whose source is not obvious from the text.

Chapter 2

Spinelli called the Single Act a 'dead mouse' in his speech to the European Parliament on 16 January 1986, reprinted in Altiero Spinelli, *Discorsi al Parlamento Europeo*, ed. Pier Virgilio Dastoli (Bologna, 1987), p. 369. Jenkins recalled his choice of a theme to 'move Europe forward' in *European Diary 1977–1981* (London, 1989), pp. 22–3.

Chapter 3

Margaret Thatcher spoke of 'a European super-state' in her *Britain and Europe: Text of the Speech Delivered in Bruges by the Prime Minister on 20th September 1988* (London: Conservative Political Centre, 1988), p. 4.

Chapter 7

Bevin and Victoria Station is to be found in Michael Charlton, *The Price of Victory* (London, 1983), pp. 43–4.

Chapter 9

Poos on 'the hour of Europe' was reported in the *New York Times*, 29 June 1991, p. 4.

Chapter 10

The Community 'as an example' is from Jean Monnet, *Les États-Unis d'Europe ont commencé: Discours et allocutions 1952–1954* (Paris, 1955), p. 128.

The EC as 'the most important member of Gatt' is from Lawrence B. Krause, *European Economic Integration and the United States* (Washington, DC, 1968), p. 225.

The EC and 'effective international law-making' is from Tommaso Padoa-Schioppa, *Financial and Monetary Integration in Europe: 1990, 1992 and Beyond* (London and New York, 1990), p. 28.

Further reading

There is a great deal of academic literature on the European Union, but not so many reliable books for the general reader or for those who are just setting out to acquire academic knowledge.

Of the many texts that provide **general introductions**, two good options are Desmond Dinan's *Ever Closer Union* (Basingstoke, 4th edn, 2010, 640 pp.) and John McCormick's *Understanding the EU* (Basingstoke, 5th edn, 2011, 264 pp.). A federalist view of the way in which the EU has developed is to be found in Michael Burgess, *Federalism and European Union: The Building of Europe, 1950–2000* (London, 2000, 290 pp.). Chapters on all the main policies are to be found in Helen Wallace, Mark Pollack, and Alisdair Young (eds), *Policy-Making in the European Union* (Oxford, 6th edn, 2010, 640 pp.). A wide range of subjects is also covered in the *Annual Review* of the *Journal of Common Market Studies* (Oxford).

Timothy Bainbridge and Anthony Teasdale, *The Penguin Companion to the European Union* (Harmondsworth, 3rd edn, 2012, 880 pp.) is an accurate and convenient **work of reference**. For those who appreciate a **biographical** approach to the subject, the history of the EC up to the 1970s is seen through the eyes of its principal founding father in Jean Monnet's *Memoirs* (London, 1978, 544 pp.). Flavour and substance of the Delors period, from 1985 to 1994, are to be found in Charles Grant, *Inside the House that Jacques Built* (London, 1994, 305 pp.). A range of leading actors in the uniting of Europe are given lively treatment in Martyn Bond, Julie Smith, and William Wallace (eds), *Eminent Europeans* (London, 1996, 321 pp.). Hugo Young provides unsurpassed insights into the development of British relations with the EU, through chapters on a dozen British protagonists and antagonists from Churchill to Blair, in *This Blessed Plot* (Basingstoke, 1998, 558 pp.).

There is not much that is easy to read and gives a true and fair view of how the **institutions** work. Neil Nugent's *The Government and Politics of the European Union* (Basingstoke, 7th edn, 2010, 512 pp.) is reliable and comprehensive, but not light reading. Michelle Cini and Nieves Perez-Solorzano Borragan's *European Union Politics* (Oxford, 3rd edn, 2010, 520 pp.) opens up a wide range of subjects to the reader. John Peterson and Michael Shackleton's *The Institutions of the European Union* (Oxford, 3rd edn, 2012, 472 pp.) is a very good overview. Shorter explanations of the institutions can be found in the chapter on 'Institutions or Constitution' in *The Building of the European Union* and in Helen Wallace's chapter on 'An Institutional Anatomy and Five Policy Modes' in Wallace, Pollack, and Young (eds), *Policy-Making in the European Union* (both books cited above). Chapters 7–10 of Dinan's *Ever Closer Union* (also cited above) deal with main institutions.

Ali El-Agraa's *The European Union: Economics and Policies* (Cambridge, 9th edn, 2011, 518 pp.) has the most current overview of **economics and economic policies**. Lord Cockfield's *The European Union: Creating the Single Market* (Chichester, 1994, 185 pp.) is a lucid and entertaining account by the man who did most to create it, while Alasdair Young, in 'The Single Market' (chapter in Wallace, Pollack, and Young (eds), *Policy-Making in the European Union*), brings you up to date. The budget is well explained by Brigid Laffan and Johannes Lindner (chapter in Wallace, Pollack, and Young (eds), *Policy-Making in the European Union*). A useful summary of the EU's environmental policies is given in Andrew Jordan and Camilla Adelle (eds), *Environmental Policy in the EU: Actors, Institutions and Processes* (Abingdon, 2012, 424 pp.).

Most of the literature on the EU's **external relations** is about the Common Foreign and Security Policy, though the external economic policies remain more effective and important. Fraser Cameron gives a wide-ranging overview in *An Introduction to European Foreign Policy* (Abingdon, 2012, 320 pp.), with Stephan Keukeleire and Jennifer MacNaughtan's more detailed *The Foreign Policy of the European Union* (Basingstoke, 2008, 392 pp.) working as a companion.

The **Area of Freedom, Security, and Justice** is also a fast-moving subject: Sandra Lavenex's chapter on 'Justice and Home Affairs' in Wallace, Pollack, and Young (eds), *Policy-Making in the European Union* gives a good overview.

Across the board, the EU's website—http://europa.eu—is a vast quarry of information, from the very basic through to the highly technical.

Chronology 1946–2013

1940s

19 September 1946	Churchill calls for 'a kind of United States of Europe'.
5 June 1947	Marshall Plan announced.
16 April 1948	EEC (later OECD) created to coordinate Marshall Plan for West European states.
4 April 1949	Signature of North Atlantic Treaty establishing Nato.
5 May 1949	Establishment of Council of Europe.

1950s

9 May 1950	Schuman Declaration launches negotiations to establish ECSC, as 'a first step in the federation of Europe'.
18 April 1951	The Six (Belgium, France, Germany, Italy, Luxembourg, Netherlands) sign ECSC Treaty.
27 May 1952	The Six sign European Defence Community (EDC) Treaty.
27 July 1952	ECSC Treaty enters into force.
30 August 1954	French National Assembly shelves EDC Treaty.
20 October 1954	The Six and UK found WEU.
1–2 June 1955	Foreign ministers of the Six agree at Messina to launch negotiations resulting in EEC and Euratom.
25 March 1957	Rome Treaties establishing EEC and Euratom signed.
1 January 1958	Rome Treaties enter into force.

1960s

3 May 1960	Efta established by Austria, Denmark, Norway, Portugal, Sweden, Switzerland, UK.
31 July, 10 August 1961	Ireland, Denmark, UK apply to join Communities. Norway applies in April 1962.
14 January 1962	Common agricultural policy agreed by the Six.
14 January 1963	President de Gaulle terminates accession negotiations.
1 July 1965	France breaks off negotiations on financing CAP, boycotts Council until January 1966.
28-9 January 1966	Luxembourg 'Compromise' agreed. France returns to Council insisting on unanimity when 'very important' interests at stake.
11 May 1967	UK reactivates membership application followed by Ireland, Denmark, Norway. De Gaulle still demurs.
1 July 1968	Customs union completed 18 months ahead of schedule.
1-2 December 1969	Hague Summit agrees arrangements for financing CAP, and resumption of accession negotiations.

1970s

22 April 1970	Amending Treaty signed, giving Community all revenue from common external tariff and agricultural import levies plus share of value-added tax, and European Parliament some powers over budget.
27 October 1970	Council establishes 'EPC' procedures for foreign policy cooperation.
22 March 1971	Council adopts plan to achieve Emu by 1980, soon derailed by international monetary turbulence.
22 January 1972	Accession Treaties of Denmark, Ireland, Norway, UK signed (but Norwegians reject theirs in referendum).
1 January 1973	Denmark, Ireland, UK join Community.
9-10 December 1974	Paris Summit decides to hold meetings three times a year as European Council and gives go-ahead for direct elections to European Parliament.
28 February 1975	Community and 46 African, Caribbean, and Pacific countries sign Lomé Convention.

18 March 1975	European Regional Development Fund established.
22 July 1975	Amending Treaty signed, giving European Parliament more budgetary powers and setting up Court of Auditors.
4–5 December 1978	European Council establishes European Monetary System with Exchange Rate Mechanism based on ecu.
7, 10 June 1979	First direct elections to European Parliament.

1980s

1 January 1981	Greece becomes tenth member of Community.
14 February 1984	Draft Treaty on European Union, inspired by Spinelli, passed by big majority in European Parliament.
25–6 June 1984	Fontainebleau European Council agrees on rebate to reduce UK's net contribution to Community budget.
7 January 1985	New Commission takes office, Delors President.
14 June 1985	Schengen Agreement eliminating border controls signed by Belgium, France, Germany, Luxembourg, Netherlands.
28–9 June 1985	European Council approves Commission project to complete single market by 1992; considers proposals from Parliament's Draft Treaty; initiates IGC for Treaty amendment.
1 January 1986	Spain, Portugal accede, membership now 12.
17, 28 February 1986	Single European Act signed.
1 July 1987	Single European Act enters into force.
1 July 1988	Interinstitutional Agreement between Parliament, Council, Commission on budgetary discipline and procedure enters into force.
24 October 1988	Court of First Instance established.
9 November 1989	Fall of Berlin Wall. German Democratic Republic opens borders.
8–9 December 1989	European Council initiates IGC on Emu; all save UK adopt charter of workers' social rights.

1990s

| 28 April 1990 | European Council agrees policy on German unification and relations with Central and East European states. |

29 May 1990	Agreement signed to establish European Bank for Reconstruction and Development.
19 June 1990	Second Schengen Agreement signed.
20 June 1990	EEC and Efta start negotiations to create European Economic Area (EEA).
25–6 June 1990	European Council decides to call IGC on political union, parallel with that on Emu.
3 October 1990	Unification of Germany and de facto enlargement of Community.
14–15 December 1990	European Council launches IGCs on Emu and political union.
9–10 December 1991	European Council agrees TEU (Maastricht Treaty).
16 December 1991	'Europe Agreements' with Poland, Hungary, Czechoslovakia signed; those with Czech Republic and Slovakia (successors to Czechoslovakia), Bulgaria, Estonia, Latvia, Lithuania, Romania, Slovenia follow at intervals.
7 February 1992	Maastricht Treaty signed.
2 May 1992	Agreement on EEA signed.
2 June 1992	Danish referendum rejects Maastricht Treaty.
20 September 1992	French referendum narrowly approves Maastricht Treaty.
6 December 1992	Swiss referendum rejects joining EEA; attempt to join EU shelved.
11–12 December 1992	European Council offers Denmark special arrangements to facilitate Treaty ratification; endorses Delors package of budgetary proposals; agrees to start accession negotiations with Austria, Norway, Sweden, Finland.
31 December 1992	Bulk of single market legislation completed on time.
18 May 1993	Second Danish referendum accepts Maastricht Treaty.
21–2 June 1993	Copenhagen European Council declares associated Central and East European states can join when they fulfil the political and economic conditions.
1 November 1993	Maastricht Treaty enters into force.
28 November 1994	Norwegian referendum rejects accession.

1 January 1995	Austria, Finland, Sweden join, membership now 15.
12 July 1995	European Parliament appoints first Union Ombudsman.
26 July 1995	Member states sign Europol Convention.
31 December 1995	EC–Turkey customs union enters into force.
29 March 1996	IGC to revise Maastricht Treaty begins.
2 October 1997	Amsterdam Treaty signed.
12 March 1998	Accession negotiations open with Cyprus, Czech Republic, Estonia, Hungary, Poland, Slovenia.
3 May 1998	Council decides 11 states ready to adopt euro on 1 January 1999.
1 June 1998	European Central Bank established.
24–5 October 1998	European Council agrees measures of defence cooperation.
31 December 1998	Council fixes irrevocable conversion rates between euro and currencies of participating states.
1 January 1999	Euro becomes official currency of Austria, Belgium, Finland, France, Germany, Ireland, Italy, Luxembourg, Netherlands, Portugal, Spain.
15 March 1999	Commission resigns following report by independent committee on allegations of mismanagement and fraud.
1 May 1999	Amsterdam Treaty enters into force.
10–11 December 1999	European Council decides on accession negotiations with six more states; recognizes Turkey as applicant; initiates IGC for Treaty revision.

2000s

15 January 2000	Accession negotiations open with Bulgaria, Latvia, Lithuania, Malta, Romania, Slovakia.
20 June 2000	Lisbon European Council agrees measures for flexibility in EU economy.
28 September 2000	Danish voters reject membership of euro in referendum.
7–10 December 2000	European Council concludes negotiations for Nice Treaty and solemnly proclaims the Charter of Fundamental Rights.
1 January 2001	Greece becomes 12th member of the Eurozone.

7 June 2001	Irish voters reject Treaty of Nice in a referendum.
14–15 December 2001	Laeken European Council agrees declaration on future of Union, opening way for a wholesale reform process.
1 January 2002	Euro notes and coins enter into circulation.
28 February 2002	Convention on the Future of the EU opens in Brussels.
19 October 2002	Irish voters approve Treaty of Nice in a second referendum.
12–13 December 2002	Copenhagen European Council concludes accession negotiations with ten countries in Central and Eastern Europe and the Mediterranean.
1 February 2003	Treaty of Nice enters into force.
14 September 2003	Swedish voters reject membership of euro in a referendum.
4 October 2003	IGC opens to consider treaty reform on basis of Convention's draft EU constitution.
1 May 2004	Cyprus, Czech Republic, Estonia, Hungary, Latvia, Lithuania, Malta, Poland, Slovakia, and Slovenia join the Union, making 25 member states.
29 June 2004	Barroso nominated new Commission President.
29 October 2004	Heads of State and Government and the EU Foreign Ministers sign the Treaty establishing a Constitution for Europe.
29 May, 1 June 2005	French and Dutch voters reject Constitutional Treaty in referendums.
3 October 2005	Accession negotiations open with Turkey and Croatia.
1 January 2007	Bulgaria and Romania become the 26th and 27th member states of the Union. Slovenia becomes the 13th participant in Eurozone.
23 July 2007	Opening of IGC on Lisbon Treaty.
13 December 2007	Signing of Lisbon Treaty.
21 December 2007	Enlargement of Schengen area to Estonia, Czech Republic, Lithuania, Hungary, Latvia, Malta, Poland, Slovakia, and Slovenia.
1 January 2008	Cyprus and Malta adopt euro.
12 June 2008	Irish voters reject Lisbon Treaty in referendum.

15 October 2008	Brussels European Council sets out first response to global financial crisis.
12 December 2008	Switzerland joins Schengen area.
1 January 2009	Slovakia joins euro.
4–7 June 2009	European Parliament elections.
23 July 2009	Iceland applies for EU membership.
3 October 2009	Irish voters vote in favour of Lisbon Treaty in referendum.
20 November 2009	Appointment of Herman van Rompuy as first President of the European Council and of Catherine Ashton as High Representative of the Union for Foreign Affairs and Security Policy.
1 December 2009	Lisbon Treaty enters into force.
2010s	
17 June 2010	Adoption of 'Europe 2020' strategy for sustainable growth over next 10 years.
1 January 2011	Estonia adopts the euro. Start of operations for new financial supervisory bodies: the European Banking Authority, the European Securities and Markets Authority, and the European Insurance and Occupational Pensions Authority.
18 January 2011	Start of first 'European semester' of economic policy coordination by member states.
25 March 2011	Euro Plus Pact agreed.
11 July 2011	Eurozone members sign treaty on European Stability Mechanism, to act as a reserve for states in financial crisis.
21 July 2011	First round of support for Greek economy of €109 billion.
1 November 2011	Mario Draghi becomes new President of the ECB.
8 November 2011	Adoption of 'sixpack' legislation on economic governance.
30 January 2012	New treaty on Stability, Coordination, and Governance is agreed by all member states except the Czech Republic and the UK.
21 February 2012	Second round of support for Greek economy.
1 March 2012	Serbia given candidate status.
1 April 2012	European Citizens' Initiative comes into force, enabling citizens to propose EU legislation.
1 July 2013	Croatia becomes 28th member state.

Glossary

Words in *italics* refer to other entries.

Accession: The process of joining the *European Union*. After accession treaties have been negotiated, all member states must ratify them and the European Parliament must give its assent.

Acquis Communautaire: The full set of the *European Union*'s legislative, regulatory, judicial, and normative output.

Amsterdam Treaty: See *Treaty of Amsterdam*.

Area of Freedom, Security, and Justice (AFSJ): Policies relating to coordination of internal security and justice systems.

Asymmetric shocks: Affect different regions within an economy in different ways: a potential problem for the *Eurozone*.

Budget of the European Union: Revenue comes from *own resources*; two-thirds of spending is on the *common agricultural* and *cohesion* policies.

Citizenship: The *Treaty on European Union* created a European citizenship, alongside member states' citizenships. Citizens are entitled to rights conferred by the treaties.

Cohesion policy: The *European Union*'s regional development policy, implemented through *structural funds* accounting for one-third of European Union *budget* spending.

Comitology: System of committees of member states' officials supervising the *Commission*'s work on behalf of the *Council*. Now largely replaced by *implementing acts*.

Commission, European Commission: The main executive body of the *European Union*, comprising 28 Commissioners, responsible for different policy areas. In addition to its executive functions, the Commission initiates legislation and supervises compliance. The term 'Commission' is often used collectively for the Commission and its staff.

Committee of Permanent Representatives (Coreper): See *Council*.

Committee of the Regions: Comprises representatives of regional and local authorities. Provides opinions on legislation and issues reports on its own initiative.

Common agricultural policy (CAP): Much reformed, it still accounts for 40 per cent of the EU's budget spending, through its direct support of farmers and rural development.

Common Foreign and Security Policy (CFSP): Originally the second *pillar* of the *European Union*, for intergovernmental cooperation on foreign policy. Now an integral part of the *Union*.

Common Security and Defence Policy (CSDP): The defence and military cooperation element of *CFSP*.

Community: See *European Community*.

Constitutional Treaty: A proposed treaty revision, based on the work of the *Convention on the Future of Europe*, but rejected following referendums in 2005 in France and the Netherlands, despite ratification by the majority of member states. Most of its provisions were eventually incorporated into the *Lisbon Treaty*.

Convention on the Future of Europe: Open forum of representatives of parliaments and governments set up in 2002 after the Laeken declaration by the *European Council* to discuss a complete redrawing of the EU. Under its chair, Valéry Giscard d'Estaing, it presented a Draft Treaty establishing a Constitution for Europe in 2003, which formed the basis of the *Constitutional Treaty*.

Cooperation in Justice and Home Affairs (CJHA): Former third *pillar* of the *European Union*, for cooperation relating to movement of people across frontiers and for combating cross-frontier crime.

Copenhagen Criteria: The benchmarks used by the EU for evaluating the suitability of states applying for membership. They cover: stable institutions guaranteeing democracy, the rule of law, human rights and respect for minorities; a functioning market economy; the ability to take on the *acquis* and support for the various aims of the *European Union*.

Council, Council of Ministers: Comprises representatives of member states at ministerial level. It amends and *votes* on legislation, supervises execution of policies. It is supported by the Council Secretariat in Brussels, and by the Committee of Permanent Representatives and its system of committees (see *Comitology*). The Council, with the *European Council*, is the *European Union's* most powerful political institution.

Court of Justice: The final judicial authority with respect to *Union* law. Its 28 judges, one from each member state sitting in Luxembourg, have developed extensive case law (see *European legal order*). The Court has ensured that the rule of law prevails in the *Union*.

Direct effect: See *European legal order*.

Directive: A *Union* legal act that is 'binding, as to the result to be achieved', but leaves to member states' authorities 'the choice of form and methods'.

Economic and Monetary Union (Emu): Seventeen member states participate in Emu, having satisfied the 'convergence criteria' of sound finance and irrevocably fixed their exchange rates with the euro, which replaced their currencies at the beginning of 2002. Monetary policy is the responsibility of the *European Central Bank* and the *European System of Central Banks*. There is a system for coordination of economic policy.

Economic and Social Committee (Ecosoc): Comprises representatives of employers, workers, and social groups. Provides opinions on *Union* legislation and issues reports on its own initiative.

Electoral systems: In elections to the *European Parliament*, proportional representation is now used in all countries, since the UK adopted it for the 1999 elections.

Enhanced cooperation: Allows those states that want to integrate more closely than others in particular fields to do so within the *European Union* framework.

European Atomic Energy Community (Euratom): Established in 1957 alongside the *European Economic Community* to promote cooperation in the field of atomic energy; undertakes research and development for civilian purposes.

European Central Bank (ECB): Responsible for monetary policy for the Eurozone. Based in Frankfurt, the ECB is run by an Executive Board. Its members and the governors of central banks in the

Eurozone comprise ECB's Governing Council. ECB and central banks together form the European System of Central Banks (ESCB), whose primary objective is to maintain price stability. None of these participants may take instructions from any other body.

European Coal and Steel Community (ECSC): Launched by the Schuman Declaration of 9 May 1950, placing coal and steel sectors of six states (Belgium, France, Germany, Italy, Luxembourg, Netherlands) under a system of common governance. The *European Economic Community* and *Euratom* were based on the ECSC's institutional structure. The treaty lapsed in 2002.

European Commission: See *Commission*.

European Community (EC): The central *pillar* of the *European Union*, as laid out in the *Maastricht Treaty*. Incorporating the *European Economic Community*, the *European Coal and Steel Community*, and *Euratom*, it contained federal elements of the *European Union* institutions and was responsible for the bulk of European Union activities. With the *Lisbon Treaty*, the EC is now fully integrated with the rest of the *Union*.

European Convention on Human Rights and Fundamental Freedoms: A framework for the protection of human rights across Europe, adopted in 1950 by the Council of Europe. *European Union* states are all signatories and it is a basis for the respect of human rights in the European Union. The EU's Charter of Fundamental Rights is based in large part on the Convention.

European Council: Comprises the President of the European Council, Heads of State and Government of the member states, and President of the *Commission*. Takes decisions that require resolution or impetus at that level and defines political guidelines for the *European Union*.

European Court of Justice (ECJ): See *Court of Justice*.

European Defence Community (EDC): A bold attempt in the early 1950s to integrate the armed forces of the *European Coal and Steel Community* states, shelved by the French National Assembly.

European Economic Community (EEC): Established in 1958 by the *Treaty of Rome*, its competences included the creation of a common market among the six member states and wide-ranging economic policy cooperation. Its main institutions were the *Commission*, *Council, European Parliament, Court of Justice*. It is the basis for today's *European Union*.

European legal order: The *Court of Justice* has established key principles of Community law. One is 'direct effect', enabling individuals to secure their rights under Community law in the same way as member states' laws. Another is 'primacy' of Community law, ensuring it is evenly applied throughout the Community.

European Monetary System (EMS): A precursor of *Economic and Monetary Union*, its key element was the Exchange Rate Mechanism, limiting exchange rate fluctuations.

European Parliament (EP): The directly elected body of the *European Union*, its *Members* (MEPs) have substantial powers over *legislation*, the *budget*, and the *Commission*.

European Political Cooperation (EPC): Intergovernmental foreign policy cooperation, introduced in 1970 and replaced in 1993 by the *Common Foreign and Security Policy*.

European Stability Mechanism (ESM): The permanent body set up in 2012 to provide emergency financial support to *Eurozone* member states in economic difficulty.

European System of Central Banks (ESCB): See *European Central Bank*.

European Union (EU): Created by the *Treaty on European Union*, with two new *pillars* alongside the central *Community* pillar, for cooperation in foreign and security policy and in 'justice and home affairs'. While the three pillars shared common institutions, the two new ones were predominantly intergovernmental. Since the *Lisbon Treaty*, the pillars are collapsed into one, with some residual differences in procedures between policy areas.

Eurozone: The area covered by the euro, the *Union*'s single currency.

Federation: A federal polity is one in which the functions of government are divided between democratic institutions at two or more levels. The powers are usually divided according to the principle of *subsidiarity*, the member states or constituent parts having those powers that they can manage effectively.

Fiscal Compact: The 2012 treaty signed outside the *Union*'s legal order between most member states to enshrine balanced national budgets, with oversight by the *Commission*. Formally called the Treaty on Stability, Coordination, and Governance in the Economic and Monetary Union (TSCG).

Free movement: The treaties provide for free movement within the *European Union* of people, goods, capital, and services, known as 'the four freedoms'.

General Court: Judges cases brought by individuals, as well as those relating to competition policy, trademark law, and state aids.

Implementing Acts: The system for oversight of implementation of *Union* legislation by member states, as introduced by the *Lisbon Treaty*.

Intergovernmental Conference (IGC): The main way in which the *European Union*'s treaties are revised. Member states' representatives in the IGC draft an amending treaty, which must be ratified by each state before it enters into force.

Legislative procedures: Most *European Union* laws are enacted under the Ordinary Legislative Procedure, giving both *European Parliament* and *Council* powers to accept, amend, or reject legislation. The cooperation procedure, which gave the EP less power, is no longer important; but the consultation procedure, where EP is merely informed of Council's intentions, is still quite widely applicable. The consent (formerly assent) procedure gives EP powers over accession treaties, association agreements, and some legislative matters.

Lisbon Treaty: See *Treaty of Lisbon*.

Maastricht Treaty: See *Treaty on European Union*.

Members of the European Parliament (MEPs): Currently 751 MEPs are elected to the *European Parliament* from across the member states. MEPs represent their constituents; scrutinize legislation in committees; vote on laws and the budget; supervise the *Commission*; debate the range of *European Union* affairs.

Nice Treaty: See *Treaty of Nice*.

North Atlantic Treaty Organization (Nato): Founded in 1949 as the security umbrella for Western Europe, tying in the US to the European security system.

Open method of coordination: An increasingly common means of getting member states to share information and best practices without the use of legislation.

Own resources: The tax revenue for the *budget of the European Union*. The main sources are percentages of member states' GNPs and of the base for value-added tax; smaller amounts come from external tariffs and agricultural import levies.

Permanent representations: Each member state has a permanent representation in Brussels, which is a centre for its interaction with the *European Union*. The head of the representation is the state's representative in Coreper (see *Council*).

Petersberg tasks: The military and security priorities for the EU's foreign policy. They include humanitarian and rescue tasks; peacekeeping; and crisis management.

Pillars: The *Maastricht Treaty* set up the *European Union* using a pillar system. The central pillar was the *European Community* and the other two were for the *Common Foreign and Security Policy* and *Police and Judicial Cooperation in Criminal Matters* (originally known as *Cooperation in Justice and Home Affairs*). The *Lisbon Treaty* collapsed all three pillars into the *Union*.

Police and Judicial Cooperation in Criminal Matters: See *Cooperation in Justice and Home Affairs*.

Presidency: The *Council* is chaired by representatives of one of the member states, on a six-month rotating basis.

Primacy: See *European legal order*.

Qualified majority voting (QMV): See *voting*.

Regulation: A *European Community* legal act that is 'binding in its entirety and directly applicable' in all member states.

Schengen Agreements: Originating in 1985 outside the *European Union*, the Schengen Agreements now cover all member states save Ireland, the UK, and to some extent Denmark. The Agreements have been incorporated in the *European Union*.

Secondary legislation: Laws enacted by the institutions within the powers given them by the treaties.

Single European Act (SEA): Signed in 1986, the first major reform of the Rome Treaty. It provided for the 1992 programme to complete the single market; added some new competences; extended the use of qualified majority *voting*; enhanced the role of the *European Parliament*.

Structural funds: Cohesion Fund, Regional Development Fund, Social Fund (see *Cohesion policy*).

Subsidiarity: A principle requiring action to be taken at *European Union* level only when it can be more effective than action by individual states.

Treaties of Rome: See *European Economic Community* and *European Atomic Energy Community*. The EEC Treaty is often called 'the Treaty of Rome'.

Treaty of Amsterdam: Signed in 1997, it extended the scope of co-decision and reformed the *pillars* on foreign policy and on justice and home affairs.

Treaty of Lisbon: Signed in 2007, it collapses the *Union*'s pillars, creates a new legal personality for the EU, revises decision-making procedures, and creates new offices for a President of the European Council and a High Representative for Foreign Affairs and Security Policy. It draws significantly on the work of the *Convention on the Future of Europe* and the failed *Constitutional Treaty*.

Treaty of Nice: Signed in 2001, the Nice Treaty provided for institutional reforms in anticipation of the enlargement to Central and Eastern Europe, with new voting weights and procedures, and more use for *enhanced cooperation* procedures.

Treaty on European Union (TEU): Signed in 1991 at Maastricht, it established the *European Union*. It laid down the procedures for creating *Economic and Monetary Union*; gave the *European Parliament* important new powers; introduced a European *citizenship*; set up two new *pillars*, for *Common Foreign and Security Policy* and *Cooperation in Justice and Home Affairs*.

Union: See *European Union*.

Voting: Most decisions in the *Council* are taken by *Qualified Majority Voting* (QMV), which requires super-majorities of member states and of population. Unanimity applies less frequently to *Union* legislation but is more common in politically sensitive fields. Voting by simple majority is rare and mainly limited to procedural matters.

Western European Union (WEU): Created in 1954 by the UK and *European Community* member states. After a long period of inaction, the *Maastricht* and *Amsterdam* Treaties provided for links between the *European Union* and WEU, which became incorporated into the EU. The WEU was declared defunct in 2011.

World Trade Organization (WTO): The 1995 successor to Gatt, WTO regulates international trade. It aims to reduce barriers to international trade and has mechanisms for resolving disputes.

Index

Page references in italics indicate illustrations and their captions.

Index

SOCIAL MEDIA
Very Short Introduction

Join our community
www.oup.com/vsi

- Join us online at the official Very Short Introductions
  Facebook page.
- Access the thoughts and musings of our authors with our
  online **blog**.
- Sign up for our monthly **e-newsletter** to receive information
  on all new titles publishing that month.
- Browse the full range of Very Short Introductions online.
- Read **extracts** from the Introductions for free.
- Visit our library of **Reading Guides**. These guides, written by our
  expert authors will help you to question again, why you think
  what you think.
- If you are a teacher or lecturer you can order inspection
  copies quickly and simply via our website.

Visit the Very Short Introductions website to access all this and
more for free.
www.oup.com/vsi

ONLINE CATALOGUE
A Very Short Introduction

Our online catalogue is designed to make it easy to find your ideal Very Short Introduction. View the entire collection by subject area, watch author videos, read sample chapters, and download reading guides.

http://fds.oup.com/www.oup.co.uk/general/vsi/index.html

GLOBALIZATION
A Very Short Introduction
Manfred Steger

'Globalization' has become one of the defining buzzwords of our time - a term that describes a variety of accelerating economic, political, cultural, ideological, and environmental processes that are rapidly altering our experience of the world. It is by its nature a dynamic topic - and this *Very Short Introduction* has been fully updated for 2009, to include developments in global politics, the impact of terrorism, and environmental issues. Presenting globalization in accessible language as a multifaceted process encompassing global, regional, and local aspects of social life, Manfred B. Steger looks at its causes and effects, examines whether it is a new phenomenon, and explores the question of whether, ultimately, globalization is a good or a bad thing.